Traditions, Institutions, and American Popular Music

Contemporary Music Review
2000, Vol. 19, Part 1, p. iii
Reprints available directly from the publisher
Photocopying permitted by license only

© 2000 OPA (Overseas Publishers Association) N.V.
Published by license under
the Harwood Academic Publishers imprint,
part of The Gordon and Breach Publishing Group.
Printed in Malaysia.

Contents

Contemporary Music Review
2000, Vol. 19, Part 1, pp. 1–4
Reprints available directly from the publisher
Photocopying permitted by license only

Preface

This issue of *Contemporary Music Review* focuses on the composers, performers, theorists, historians, critics, and listeners who welcome the potentially difficult — but also potentially fruitful — intercourse between "classical" and "popular" styles and techniques in American music and culture; this group of new essays addresses a variety of philosophical, historical, and analytical topics concerning the relationships between the learned and the vernacular in the music of this century's stage, screen, sound recordings, and academies. Taken together with its companion volume, "American Rock and the Classical Music Tradition," these essays suggest that the interaction of popular and art music in American culture not only raises a number of fascinating and even sometimes highly charged issues, but that it also has a rich history dating back at least to the end of the nineteenth century. In fact, there seems not to have been a time in the last one hundred years when American musicians were not experimenting with some kind of pop-art music fusion; a brief chronological list spanning the century might include such diverse figures as Scott Joplin, George Gershwin, Gunther Schuller, Milton Babbitt, and Frank Zappa.

While the essays in "American Rock and the Classical Music Tradition" argue that the interaction of art-music and rock can be very compelling and fruitful in American pop since the 1960s, the idea of blending classical music with pop was already a part of American culture by the time the rockers got to it. The essays in this collection by Allen Forte, David Neumeyer, and David Joyner explore this interaction in American music before 1965. In "Harmonic Relations: American Popular Harmonies (1925–1950) and Their European Kin," Allen Forte illuminates the surprisingly close relationships between the avant-garde European art music of the first quarter of this century and the American popular ballad of the second, particularly as heard in the content, colors, and functions of harmonic sonorities. Individual harmonies normally associated with the atonal contexts of works by Schoenberg, Webern, and Berg are found comfortably nestled within the contrastingly tonal contexts of songs by Gershwin, Kern, and Berlin.

Forte considers these sonorities with regard to the effectual qualities and functional roles of their constituent intervals, noting the ways in which similar vertical combinations can be at once so alike while also very different.

David Neumeyer examines a domain of popular music from this same era (mostly concentrating on the decade of 1926–35), but one created to totally different ends, in "Performances in Early Hollywood Sound Films: Source Music, Background Music, and the Integrated Sound Track." After discussing the narrative roles played in various portions of the musical space in soundtracks from this era, and challenging the frequent and snobby privileging of the symphonic background score over popular "source" music (such as the entertainment-motivated songs featured in acted performances), Neumeyer offers a model for analyzing the integrated soundtrack that permits far greater subtlety of distinction than current models, based on a binary diegetic/non-diegetic model, allow. He illustrates his method with an extended analysis of fifteen minutes from the "Café americaine" scene (including Sam's performance of "As Time Goes By") from *Casablanca* (1943).

Whereas the jazz world is touched on in a number the essays in this volume, it takes center stage in David Joyner's "Analyzing Third Stream." Focusing on the relationship between improvisation and "considered" composition, Joyner examines the goals and claims made for third-stream music by its chief spokesperson, Gunther Schuller. Joyner traces various attempts to blend jazz and classical music as far back as turn-of-the-century ragtime, and follows such attempts through to the mid 1940s, the period during which third stream was developed. In many ways, third stream attempted to do within jazz what figures like Zappa and the progressive rockers tried to accomplish within rock; during the period from about 1945 to 1965, musicians such as John Lewis, Dave Brubeck, and Stan Kenton consciously blended elements drawn from modern classical music into a jazz setting (Kenton even referred to his music as "progressive jazz"). But the proponents of third stream had a very hard go of it, fighting aesthetic battles both within the jazz world and with advocates of classical music. In fact, Joyner argues that third stream was largely a failure; the problem for Joyner lies in the fact that third-stream music (for the most part) does not swing, as well as in the way in which the complicated compositional structures inhibit the freedom of the jazz improvisor.

In the course of exploring the cultural issues at stake in the fusion of jazz and classical-music cultures, Joyner's essay brings up a number of issues that have to do with the institutional structure of American musical culture. Joyner notes, for instance, that until relatively recently a Black American trained in the European tradition was not likely to be welcome in a major symphony orchestra in the United States. Similar kinds of socio-economic, racial, and cultural forces that can operate in colleges and universities are central to "Into the Ivory Tower: Vernacular Music and the American Academy" by Austin B. Caswell and Christopher Smith. Caswell and Smith discuss the academy's historical, cultural, and political resistance to the inclusion of four genres of utilitarian music — those involving chorus, band, jazz ensemble, and piano solo — and examine how such resistance was overcome by the academics' transformation of musical practice into absolute objects for aesthetic contemplation, promoting the canonization of certain works, and repressing of the subjective processes that produced them. The academic transformation, say Caswell and Smith, affects not only the evaluation of musical works, but also their identities, as perfectionism of performance technique, for instance, is substituted for once-vital creative impulses. (It seems that such an argument could also be applied to the adoption of rock repertoire into the realms of Muzak and the pops orchestra.)

Caswell and Smith's story is largely one of how music is transformed when it is assimilated into an institution, and this reading views such transformations as transgressive, opportunistic, and distortive. But it can sometimes happen that bringing a new style of music into an institution can have a markedly positive impact. Dave Headlam provides a listening guide that chronicles one such instance of this in his "Re-Drawing Boundaries: The Kronos Quartet." The Kronos ensemble can be given a great deal of credit for redefining traditional notions of the string quartet, largely due to their adaptation of rock music and performance practice (the very kind of thing, we may recall, about which Harbison complains so bitterly). Headlam surveys the group's cross-cultural tastes and argues that the resulting blend does not represent a postmodernist statement (a tag often applied to the group), but rather constitutes a thoroughly modernist one.

The collection concludes with some brief remarks by composer William Bolcom. Bolcom is, of course, well known for his championing of American popular music within art-music culture. Here he reflects on marketing forces, the bond between performer and audience, and the rise of rap music. This volume thus ends as its companion volume began: with remarks on popular music from one of America's foremost contemporary-music composers.

Taken together then, the essays in this current issue of *Contemporary Music Review* suggest that the problems of blending together popular and classical music are more complex than they might at first seem. While the tension that exists between popular and art music is not a particularly American problem, it is a problem with a rich history in American musical culture. We hope these essays, along with those from "American

Rock and the Classical Music Tradition," go some distance toward an understanding of the myriad issues that such cultural crossover can raise.

John Covach
Chapel Hill, NC

Walter Everett
Ann Arbor, MI

Contemporary Music Review
2000, Vol. 19, Part 1, pp. 5–36
Reprints available directly from the publisher
Photocopying permitted by license only

Harmonic Relations: American Popular Harmonies (1925–1950) and Their European Kin

Allen Forte

With reference to the repertoire of European avant-garde music that emerged in the early twentieth century and to the American popular music of the "golden" period 1925–1950, the article examines correspondences between specific classes of harmonies, partially interpreted as pitch-class sets, primarily in terms of their total interval content, with attention given to musical contexts of small scale.

KEYWORDS: American music, popular music, atonal music, popular harmony, atonal harmony

I. Introduction

This article explores intersections between the avant-garde music of early twentieth-century Europe and the autochthonous American popular ballad, links between the two seemingly disparate repertoires of music that are apparent in the domain of harmony. I regard this study as part of a much larger study that would encompass the etymology of tonal harmony in American vernacular art music, including jazz. The present instalment is restricted to the American popular ballad of the wonderfully creative period 1925–1950, while the remarkable European music to which I will refer stems from the preceding quarter century.

The harmonies of American popular music are sometimes regarded as distortions, through processes of accretion and chromatic alteration, of the traditional harmonies of Classical European art music, that gave rise to characteristically American idioms. Sometimes these jazz-influenced harmonies were quasi-ironic, "thumbing their noses" at classical harmonies. This is especially the case with the chord of the added sixth, which is often regarded (perhaps incorrectly) as the hallmark of the American idiom. But of course there is more to it, and therefore this article undertakes to explore some of the connections between American popular music and European avant-garde art music, another major repertoire in which harmonic innovation and metamorphosis were prominent features.

The extent of the departure from tradition that accompanied the European avant-garde movement was recognized by contemporary writers associated with it. In 1925 (the year in which the twelve-tone system of Schoenberg became firmly established and the year in which the new and demonstrably "American" features began to pervade the songs of the New York musical theatre), Schoenberg's student Erwin Stein, writing about the weakening of tonality and its replacement by the twelve-tone row as organizing principle, proclaimed: "Harmonically, above all, that meant an enormous enrichment." And further on: "While the old harmony ... recognized only a few dozen chords, henceforth all simultaneities, even those comprising all twelve tones, became possible." [1]

Of course nothing like this expansion of harmonic vocabulary occurred in American popular music, not only because, unlike the European avant-garde music, it remained under the aegis of tonality, but also because there were no "music-revolutionary" forces in motion comparable to those that flourished abroad, especially in pre-World War I *Mitteleuropa*.[2] Popular music still had to meet certain commercial standards, based upon what were assumed to be criteria of audience receptivity. Even so, there was a considerable degree of liberation from classical harmonies; more specifically, the harmonic vocabulary expanded to include new sonorities, many of which reflected the infusion of jazz elements. Indeed, because American popular music and American jazz have been so beautifully and intimately intertwined in a complex symbiotic act over such a long period, I have not hesitated to introduce examples from jazz performance here and there in the present article, beginning with the following.

Figure 1a, a latter-day instance of an "atonal" sonority in a jazz piano styling, provides perspective. Compared with the sonority in figure 1b, figure 1a is identical with respect to pitch-class set class: both are instances of hexachord 6-z17, one of Webern's favorites.[3] Not only that, but they are identical with respect to pitch-class content.[4] Here of course the situation is complex, since the Evans sonority is part of an unnotated improvisation on a popular song (Cole Porter's "What Is This Thing Called Love") written in 1932, whereas the Webern counterpart is a vertical

6-z17:[e♭,e♮,f,g,b♭,b♮]

Figure 1 Bill Evans and Anton Webern

detail in an extraordinary avant-garde composition (Opus 6/4) that had no evident antecedents or external referents. Moreover, the Evans sonority represents an extension — "intensification" is a better word — of processes that began to develop in jazz about the time Porter wrote "What Is This Thing Called Love," hence is historically remote from the Webern music, composed in 1909.

Nevertheless, the correspondences are quite remarkable, apart from the shared pitch-class content. For example, both voicings isolate the E♭-major triad as a contiguous subset, perhaps showing a common concern for that tonal artifact, and by registral disposition both emphasize E and F of the special trichord B-E-F. The latter type of trichord (3-5) is a hallmark of the Second Viennese School, to be found everywhere in Schoenberg's atonal music. In jazz and in the American popular song, the sonority usually has a dominant function, representing the third, seventh, and added sixth ("thirteenth") of a dominant harmony, with elided root. Here, at the beginning of Evans's improvisation, it is part of a chord that embellishes the first chord ("C⁷") in "What Is This Thing Called Love."[5] The total sonority of the hexachord type (6-z17) in this example, is unique, insofar as it embodies every one of the twelve possible trichords, hence is particularly rich in sound. Evans's piano spacing clearly sets off the non-interlocking trichords on top and bottom, while Webern's orchestral deployment distributes the notes among the woodwinds as shown in example 1 at c), so that the trichordal components are not as audible as they are in the Evans arrangement.

Other connections between the American and European music transcend individual harmonies, thus exceeding the scope of the present article. One instance, however, is worth citing. The central harmonies (representing keys) of the bridge of Gershwin's "How Long Has This Been Going On" are C major and B minor, and these constituents can be heard in the striking form of the dominant harmony that begins the refrain.[6] Similar processes of fragmentation and assimilation can be heard in the music of the avant-garde European composers, for example, in the Lieder, Opus 2 of Berg (1909). In the remainder of this article, however, I will concentrate on correspondences of individual harmonic sonorities and reserve such larger constructs for attention at some later date.[7]

One large issue cannot be avoided, however: why is it that although certain sonorities are common to both repertoires, it is difficult to trace a convincing common musical origin? The answer depends, as usual, on one's point of view as well as strategy. Reducing the question to the lowest common denominator we do not have to go far afield to discover that the composers of both repertoires were concerned to produce music that differed in an easily identifiable way from the traditional music of Europe. For the European avant-garde that meant music of the nineteenth century; for the American composers of popular song, who most assuredly did not regard themselves as avant-gardists, it meant the vaguely defined "classical music," composed by what Irving Berlin would have disparagingly labelled "longhairs." In the process, the best representatives of the latter group produced sophisticated and original music of small scale that often gave harmony as much attention as its age-old adversary, melody, especially in its musical depictions of agapeic travails and raptures, the verbal evocation of which was naturally limited with respect to vocabulary. (Sesquipedalian lyricists did not flourish in the field of popular music.) And of course it is precisely there that we find many of the expressive harmonic intersections of music of the two repertoires, which I have grouped into four large categories, according to basic sonic characteristics, and beginning with what many would regard as the most elemental, the achromatic.

II. Diatonic-Pentatonic Sonorities

Although we tend to think of the harmonic vocabulary of the European avant-garde as consisting of sonorities outside the familiar diatonic sphere, it does include harmonies that originated in traditional diatonic music. One such sonority is formed in the opening bars of Part II of Schoenberg's *Gurre-Lieder*, where the two-note bass figure d-f# joins the motivic F#-minor triad associated with Tove to create the major-seventh chord that dominates the opening of this music (figure 2).[8] Here we have a harmony whose predecessors originated in a diatonic context and that is now elevated to the status of a contextually independent sonority — in a frequently misapplied word, "atonal."

Figure 2   Arnold Schoenberg, *Gurre-Lieder*

In the later music of the Second Viennese School, especially in Berg's, the major-seventh sonority occurs often. The opening chord of Marie's Lullaby in *Wozzeck* is reducible to a harmony of this type (figure 3).

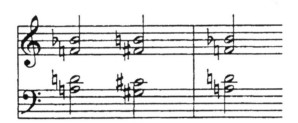

Figure 3   Alban Berg

Here in figure 3 an inverted major-seventh chord alternates with a pentatonic construct g#-c#-f#-b, supporting the unforgettable incipit of the lullaby: "Mädel, was fangst Du jetzt an?" (Girl, what are you doing?). Later on, the same type of sonority initiates the music the precedes the ominous appearance of the protagonist (figure 4), this time with the pitches of an F major-seventh chord, which, according to the composer, represents Marie's "endless waiting."[9]

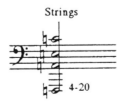

Figure 4   Alban Berg

Now, what makes the major-seventh sonority (4-20) so distinctive and sonically attractive is its perfect fifths and major thirds. Of all the tetrachords it is the only one with exactly two major thirds and two perfect fifths.[10] At the beginning of the Lullaby (figure 3) Berg arranges the chord so as to highlight the perfect fifths, placing one fifth on the bottom, the other on the top of the chord. But in its second occurrence (figure 4), the chord is rearranged so as to present one of the major thirds on the bottom (F-A) and one on the top (as the minor sixth E-C). In this way he creates a sonic association with the persona of Wozzeck, whose musical autograph e-g-b-d# belongs to the class of tetrachords that uniquely incorporates three major thirds, tetrachord 4-19.[11]

No doubt the most famous example of a major-seventh chord in the American popular song repertoire, and one to which generations of sensitive listeners have responded proleptically, occurs at the beginning of Cole Porter's "Night And Day" (figure 5).[12]

Although the major-seventh chord resolves into the dominant harmony, as shown in figure 5, its contextual origin, coming as it does from the music of the verse, is quite ambivalent, suggesting that its upper trichord, the E♭-minor triad, may be the most important constituent of the harmony (Forte 1995). It is this ambivalence, this wavering between major and minor, that reflects the opposition of "night" and "day" expressed in the title, a dualism that is present in many ways in the music of the song. In its first appearance (bar 1) the chord sets "day," but in the corresponding position in the second section of the song, bar 17, it sets "night," a beautifully sensitive reversal of the text-music relation suggested by the song title. In both instances the characteristic perfect fifths of the sonority interlock, with the lower (c♭-g♭) resolving in parallel motion to the fifth b♭-f of the dominant harmony (figure 5).

A year before Cole Porter published "Night And Day," Arthur Schwartz published his evocative, and, some would say, lubricious, song, "Dancing In The Dark," which, like the Porter, begins on a major-seventh chord (figure 6).

The lyrics of both songs evoke images of darkness and light, but the Schwartz emphasizes night and darkness, with the tenderly amorous connotations of dancing, while the Porter is a passionate and obsessive

♭VI   V

Figure 5 Cole Porter

Figure 6   Arthur Schwartz

long song. And where the music of the verse that precedes the major-seventh chord in the Porter lends it a special mystery, it is the continuation of the chord in the Schwartz that gives it such an unusually poetic quality. In effect, and as shown in Figure 6, the major-seventh chord vanishes in the diminished-seventh chord that follows it, creating a wondrous tonal image of darkness as the two characteristic perfect fifths of the major-seventh sonority collapse into the dissonant intervals of the diminished-seventh chord.[13]

Thus, although Schoenberg, Berg, Porter, and Schwartz employ the major-seventh sonority for different expressive purposes, they all utilize and emphasize its special intervallic qualities through spacing and by the vertical arrangement of its constituents, thus enhancing its unique sound by voice-leading context as well. These correspondences suggest that it is the total intervallic properties of the harmony that are of the essence, and it is this harmonic attribute that provides a firm basis for the examination of a sonority as it occurs in the two repertoires under consideration here.[14]

Within the diatonic domain, many connections between our two repertoires exist in the pentatonic sub-area — hardly a surprising statement to many readers, I am sure. Let us consider an example.

Figure 7   Claude Debussy

Debussy begins his pictorially evocative piece, "Les collines d'Anacapri," from the Préludes, Book 1 (figure 7) by delineating one of its primary melodic and harmonic constituents, the pentatonic scale, not in its commonplace ordering (beginning on e), but arranged so that the first tetrachord is a form of 4-23 (about which more below) and the last is of type 4-26, familiar in American popular music as the "chord of the added sixth" and a harmonic item coextensive with a "minor-seventh" chord. But both these labels are inappropriate here, as demonstrated by the music of bar 2 (figure 7), where all the notes of the pentatonic scale are enfolded in the simultaneity, creating 5-35, which, in terms of the contextual tonality (B major), is presumably of tonic persuasion.

In the introduction to his superb late song, "A Sleepin' Bee," Harold Arlen highlights the chord shown in figure 8. Like the chord in figure 7, this encompasses the complete pentatonic, pentad 5-35, also deploying top and bottom tetrachords as 4-23 and 4-26, but with positions reversed compared to the Debussy (compare figure 7). The lower of the two tetrachords (a♭-e♭-c-f) turns out to be the harmony upon which the melody is based, sketched in small noteheads at the right of Figure 8. But, in contrast to the asymmetric layout of the chord, the melody exploits the symmetries inherent in 4-26, beginning with the intervallic pattern (measured in semitones) 3-2-3 and then, from F, 3-4-3.

Both in the Debussy and in the Arlen, a concern for ordering and for the tetrachordal constituents that result from it is evident. And, remarkably, both highlight the "chord of the added sixth" (4-26). As I indicated above, it would probably be difficult to justify that label in the case of the Debussy. On the other hand, it is quite plausible in the Arlen, and, for once, the sheet music label, "A♭⁷," seems at least locally correct, although, as usual, it says nothing about the tonal orientation of the sonority.

Two comments are relevant in this regard. First, with respect to American popular music, the Rameauian term "chord of the added sixth" is a misleading description, for this harmony (4-26) comes to that repertoire through jazz, as a self-standing sonority, lifted intact from the pentatonic scale.[15] Second, and remarkably, the voicing of the Debussy chord sounds

Figure 8 Harold Arlen

like a contemporary jazz voicing (for example, as it might be played by pianist-vocalist Shirley Horn) and thus illustrates the continuing influence of that composer on modern American vernacular music, an influence that nevertheless has been exaggerated, as I have suggested.

Tetrachord 4-23, the archetypical "chord in fourths," is the fragment of the pentatonic probably most often encountered in the European avant-garde music of the period under consideration, often in Stravinsky (*Rite of Spring*, Mystic Circle of the Adolescents), but also in Schoenberg (Second String Quartet, Opus 10, Entrückung) and in virtually every avant-garde composer's music, with the possible exception of that of the atonal purist, Webern.

Prominent harmonic occurrences of the entire pentatonic (5-35) or of its surrogate, 4-23, in the American repertoire are rare, however. The remarkable piano introduction to Gershwin's late song, "A Foggy Day" (1937) is one instance. There the songwriter's usage is both motivic and "atmospheric," intended to invoke the sounds of Big Ben.[16] Recent jazz performers, in particular, Chick Corea, often feature the interval of the perfect fourth melodically in their improvisations. But in much of the American popular-music literature the pentatonic and its subsets and diatonic superset fulfill their most important role not in harmonies or in melodic configurations, but in the ubiquitous long-range bass progressions, the fifths-chains (sometimes called "cycles"), which dramatize the tonal orientation of many songs. In contrast, fifths-chains in the bass are rare in the atonal avant-garde repertoire, the chains at the beginning of Berg's Op. 2/1 (see below, figure 9) and at the end of his Op. 2/4 being exceptions.

III. Whole-tone formations

The whole-tone scale and its progeny infiltrate American popular song in the late 1920s and especially the early 1930s as a result of European influences. Nothing in indigenous American music (e.g., blues, gospel music) prepares this rich addition to the harmonic vocabulary.[17] No doubt Debussy is the primary but unwitting perpetrator, although here, as is the case with many of the putative "harmonic relations," there is no direct substantiating evidence. Whole-tone and whole-tone-related sonorities became prominent in some of the music of the early twentieth-century avant-garde as well, excluding Debussy as too obvious an instance. Scriabin's music may also have contributed to the proliferation of whole-tone sounds in American popular music, since his famous "mystic chord" (hexachord 6-34), one of three "almost whole-tone" hexachords, may be regarded as a hybrid whole-tone/octatonic sonority. The term octatonic and the influence of octatonic elements on American popular song will be discussed below.

4-25 3-8   4-25 4-25 3-8   4-25 3-8

Figure 9   Alban Berg

Figure 9 shows an extraordinary whole-tone passage at the very beginning of an early song by Berg, Opus 2/1. Each of the simultaneities is whole-tone in color, and all but the three trichords (3-8) are tetrachords of the same class, 4-25, which is a turbo-symmetric formation that contains the same number of major seconds, major thirds, and tritones, and intervals of no other size. Tetrachord 4-15 is so symmetric that it has only six distinct pitch-class forms. The upper three parts in figure 9 always consist of the same type of trichord (3-8), and, in the most unusual way, Berg has selected transpositions of the whole-tone chords in such a way that the bass line unfolds a long chain of fifths that sums to the C♭-major scale, the key indicated by the signature, although one is hard pressed to hear a C♭ tonality in this music because of the overriding effect of the whole-tone sonorities.

4-25:[e,f♯,a♯,c]
4-24:[a♯,c,d,f♯]

Figure 10   Ann Ronell

Beginning in the late 20s, as I noted above, the use of whole-tone sonorities in the presence of a diatonic underpinning is characteristic of many American popular songs. Figure 10, drawn from a moment in Ann Ronell's "Willow Weep For Me" (1932), provides a striking instance in which a form of the whole-tone pentad (5-33) sets the titular "me." This pentad contains both 4-25, as in the Berg, figure 9, and another, closely related tetrachord, 4-24.

4-24/4-25   5-33

Figure 11 George Gershwin

It is likely that it was Gershwin who brought the whole-tone sonorities to prominence in the American popular idiom. If he did not do this single-handedly, at least he exploited those sonorities to the extent that they became one of the hallmarks of his style, along with the pentatonic. Figure 11 shows a very prominent whole-tone sonority in a 1922 song by Gershwin, "I'll Build A Stairway To Paradise."

The harmony here (figure 11) occurs in bar 1 of the piano introduction and then elsewhere in the song. While the tonal function is that of dominant, the vertical constituents sum to a form of whole-tone tetrachord 4-24, which we heard in the song by Ann Ronell, Gershwin's protegée, written ten years later (figure 10). Here the music enters the whole-tone domain by raising the fifth of an inverted dominant seventh chord, a simple voice-leading motion, but one that effects a striking change in the harmonic surface. Moreover, when the melody changes from G to A we momentarily hear the symmetric 4-25, and the entire configuration then materializes as a five-note segment (pentad 5-33) of the whole-tone scale. When Gershwin arranged this song for his special collection, *The George Gershwin Songbook*, in 1932, he further emphasized the whole-tone color by delaying it until the last beat of the first bar, as shown at b) in figure 11.

In comparing the more extended Berg example with the snippets from Ronell and Gershwin, it seems that a common aesthetic-structural rationale underlies all three, namely, the incorporation of a pitch domain that is very remote from the diatonic-tonal on the one hand, yet which is made to co-exist with it. In the Berg the whole-tone vertical sonorities are played off against the unfolding diatonic chain of fifths — the maximum contrast within our tonal system.[18] In the Gershwin (and Ronell) the same idea prevails, but only over brief moments in the music. Nor, in general, does the American popular repertoire contain an example, as far as I know, of protracted whole-tone structure, whole-tone music that extends over longer passages, of several bars.

IV. Atonal or Extended Diatonic Harmonies

In the complex etiology of atonal harmonies it appears that some whole-tone fragments blend with diatonic sonorities to form what are sometimes called extended diatonic harmonies. Of these fragments, the most familiar is the "augmented triad," mentioned above as it occurs in its natural whole-tone habitat. A striking instance of such an atonal sonority in a diatonic-tonal context is to be found at the beginning of Cole Porter's 1939 song, "I Concentrate On You" (figure 12). This sonority, which is of type 4-19, occurs in bar 3 of the song, poignantly setting the lyric "gray." To emphasize the salient component of this chord, the "augmented triad," figure 12 shows it in isolation. Figure 13 then provides the linear context in which the harmony arises: from the major-seventh chord above bass E♭ (I), the third, g, moves by half step to f#. This chromatic note then mutates enharmonically, becoming g♭ as the third of the E♭-minor triad to create a delicate chromatic chiaroscuro that is in the service of the lyrics ("Whenever skies look gray to me And trouble begins to brew").

Tetrachord 4-19 has been characterized as the hallmark of European avant-garde atonal music of the early twentieth century, which is not surprising in view of its extraordinary internal makeup. And in the Porter example (figure 13) we hear one of the basic intervallic tensions inherent

Figure 12   Cole Porter

Figure 13   Cole Porter

in that sonority: the opposition of its augmented and minor-triad constituents. Because of the way in which 4-19 is prepared by the major-seventh sonority (figure 13), the change of one note from g to f# dramatizes the augmented triad at the top of the chord. But when the upper voice changes from d^1 to $e\flat^1$ the augmented triad dissolves into the E♭-minor triad, an entity whose emotive content, especially in juxtaposition with its major counterpart, has been rendered so potent and highly charged by centuries of tradition that explanation is hardly required.

The total harmony over all the music depicted in figure 13 is an atonal pentad, 5-21, which is to be found everywhere in Schoenberg's atonal music. Figure 14, extracted from the third movement of that composer's *Pierrot Lunaire*, provides one instance.

Figure 14   Arnold Schoenberg

Here, in a text-painting role ("lacht hell die Fontäne" — the fountain laughs brightly), we hear 5-21 in the upper register of the piano. Both bottom and top tetrachords are forms of 4-19, the only class of tetrachord represented twice within 5-21. Comparison of the Porter and Schoenberg usages reveals a significant commonality: the choice of a salient sonority (4-19) for a forcefully expressive text-setting role.

4-19   4-27

Figure 15   Alban Berg

Figure 15 displays a famous occurrence of 4-19, as part of a chord-pair (end of Act II, scene 4) that is associated with blood and with Wozzeck's forthcoming murder of his consort, Marie. By sheer coincidence, the chord comprises the same notes (pitch classes) as Cole Porter's "extended diatonic" version in figure 12. Its context and expressive role, however, are radically different. Here (figure 15) the chord collapses by half-step motion of its components into a new harmony, familiar in tonal music as a "half-diminished seventh." In this way a tonal orientation in terms of an El-minor triad, as in the Porter, is negated.[19]

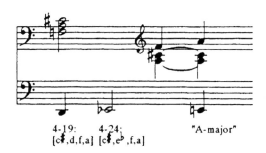

4-19:   4-24:   "A-major"
[c♯,d,f,a] [c♯,e♭,f,a]

Figure 16   Arnold Schoenberg

In figure 16 we hear 4-19 at the opening of the second song of Schoenberg's Stefan George cycle, "Fünfzehn Gedichte aus 'Das Buch der hängenden Gärten' von Stefan George," where it provides the sonorous atmosphere for the singer's description of a poetically exotic landscape. As shown in figure 16, "D-minor" implications are particularly strong. As the bass ascends by half step from D to El, the augmented triad component remains effective, transmuting 4-19 to become whole-tone tetrachord 4-24, as indicated. When the bass continues to ascend by half step and reaches E, the augmented triad's f[1] drops out, exposing an A-major triad, which might be interpreted locally as projecting a dominant function with respect to a presumed D-minor tonic. Thus, in its local voice-leading context, as an apparent bearer of traditional tonal functions, Schoenberg's 4-19 resembles Porter's in figure 12.[20]

$$V^7 \qquad I^9$$

5-30: [d♭ ,e♭ ,f,a♭ ,a♮]

Figure 17 Harold Arlen

The augmented triad remains a fixed feature in these excerpts, and, indeed, whole-tone influenced sonorities are very characteristic of many "advanced" harmonies in American popular song, especially in the music of Harold Arlen, who was perhaps the most "avant-garde" of all the songwriters of the 1925–1950 era. Figure 17 is a case in point.

The cadential dominant seventh, which occurs in a passage from Harold Arlen's 1934 song, "Ill Wind," represented schematically in figure 17, incorporates the idiomatic blue notes, a♭^{1} and d♭^{1}. This very potent sonority was definitely "state-of-the art" in popular music of that time. But like all chords of dominant function it resolves to a tonic chord, in this case the idiomatic tonic with added ninth. Regarded as an "abstract" sonority, this enriched dominant chord is an instance of pentad 5-30, whose predominant intervallic feature is the "major third" or "minor sixth," of which it possesses three instances: F-a; a-d♭^{1}; F-d♭^{1}, comprising the familiar augmented triad.[21] But the aural impact of the whole-tone component that the augmented triad represents, is offset to a considerable extent by the two fifths: e♭-a♭^{1} and d♭-a♭^{1}, so that the sonority is not as committed to the whole-tone sound, as is, say, 4-19. That tetrachord, however, is a component of 5-30 in figure 17 as F-a-d♭^{1}-a♭^{1}. Although 4-19's constituents are not all contiguous, it is very audible because the requirements of the idiom, specifically, its blues component, cause a♭^{1} to receive the melodic emphasis by virtue of its placement in the soprano, while the blue third, d♭^{1}, lies directly below it in register. Adjacent to them and in conflict with blue a♭^{1} lies a, the diatonic third of the chord. Only e♭, the seventh, stands between the upper trichord of 4-19 and bass F. The sonority is a model harmonic voicing in the American popular idiom.

No such idiomatic voicing requirements obtain in the case of 5-30 as it occurs at the very beginning of Webern's Opus 7/1, shown schematically in figure 18.

5-30:[c♯,e♭,f,g♯,a]

Figure 18   Anton Webern

Figure 18 shows 5-30 with the same pitch-class constitution as its sibling in figure 17, but the arrangement of pitches and the register of the entire sonority bring out different features, perhaps primary among which is the tritone a-e♭^{3} formed by the outer voices.[22] Now tetrachord 4-19, in all its atonal glory, occupies the middle of the sonority as f^1-a^1-c♯^{2}-g♯^{2}. But in the entire context, that sonority exhibits no voice-leading obligations, nor, indeed, does it imply a particular musical succession. In short, unlike the Arlen chord, it is a typically context-free atonal artifact.

With the extract from Webern's Opus 7/1 lingering in our ears, it seems appropriate to ask whether there are sonorities in American popular music that exhibit the "independent" character of their counterparts in atonal music. The answer is sometimes, in a way limited by the requirements of tonal syntax. The Jerome Kern excerpt in figure 19, from "All The Things You Are," is an instance.

4-19:
[e,g♯/a♭,b,c]

Figure 19   Jerome Kern

Here in figure 19 we hear the transition from the bridge to the second chorus of the song. The bridge has ended on an E-major triad, very remote (in terms of fifths) from the first harmony of the returning chorus, F minor. In the manner of a theatrical liquidation, Kern moves the fifth of the E-major triad, b, to c^1, while holding E and G# (A♭) fixed to create the augmented triad above bass A♭. The resulting total sonority is tetrachord 4-19 and, momentarily, the song is out of the control of the tonality.

Similar apophthegms are to be heard in introductions and sometimes in verses. Gershwin was given to this; for example, in the two-bar piano introduction to "Embraceable You," the second chord of which attenuates the basically dominant function of this opening music (figure 20). But in this instance blues referential elements render the E♭⁹ (♭VI) chord idiomatically American and the reassertion of the dominant-seventh chord at the end clarifies the tonal harmonic intent.

V^7 ♭VI   [V] V^7

Figure 20 George Gershwin

Two remarkable tetrachords that many readers will associate with atonal music because of their multifarious appearances in that repertoire

a)

V
4-z15:
[b♭,c,e♭,e♮]

b)

[V]
5-30:
[b♭,c,d,f♮,f♯]
4-z15:
[c,d,f♮,f♯]

Figure 21 Harold Arlen

are the all-interval tetrachords 4-z15 and 4-z29.[23] They are to be found in the American popular song repertoire as well, especially in music at the upper end of the chronological span covered in the present study. Indeed, for the next example I have gone beyond the upper limit a year or two in order to present a particularly striking example (figure 21).

If there is a single sonority that is associated with Harold Arlen's "The Man That Got Away" it is the one shown in figure 21 at a). A chord of dominant harmonic function it consists, from the bass up, of a major third, a minor seventh, and a minor third. These are but three of the six intervals of its total interval content, however. As can readily be ascertained, the remaining three intervals are a perfect fourth (E♭-B♭), a diminished fifth (B♭-E) and a diminished octave (E♭-E). When each of these tonally-defined intervals is reduced to one of the six interval classes, we find that every class is represented, exactly once (Simms 1993). From this characteristic derives the description "all-interval tetrachord."[24] It is the presence of all the interval classes that endows the sonority with its special richness and that no doubt has rendered it the object of special attention from the European avant-garde composers. Figure 21 at b) shows 4-z15 as the lower tetrachord embedded in 5-30, the opulent sonority that sets the second syllable of the titular "away." Now the upper tetrachord in 5-30 is 4-16, another sonority characteristic of both repertoires, as I will explain below.

Figure 22 at a), from *The Rite of Spring*, "Mystic Circle of the Adolescents," provides an instance of the all-interval tetrachord in its 4-z15 manifestation. At this moment in the music, the tetrachord harmonizes the first note of the movement's famous melody. In figure 22 at b) we hear 4-z15's counterpart, 4-z19, as a cadential, but entirely non-tonal, sonority in the same movement, at R99. What may give it the appearance of tonal reference is the presence of the G#-minor triad. But triads may and do occur in atonal contexts, as everyone knows.[25]

Figure 22   Igor Stravinsky

V
4-z29:
[e,f,g,b]

Figure 23   Richard Rodgers

Figure 23 presents an authentic occurrence of the all-interval tetrachord in its 4-z29 guise in a typical popular-song context as a cadential formation. The harmonic function is that of G-dominant, with both seventh and sixth present above the bass. And, as always, a "tonal" triad is one of the four triadic components of the sonority; but it is an "e-minor" triad (upper staff), which is not the tonally functional harmonic component, and thus may be regarded as not directly relevant to the tonal orientation of the song. In jazz parlance this would be a "13th" chord because of the E, but in addition to the inaccuracy and inadequacy of that description I might point out that it does not reflect the harmony's extraordinary interval content; all possible interval classes are present.

The all-interval tetrachords are often encountered in an octatonic context in the European music, but before we venture into that territory, let us consider a final case of a tetrachordal sonority common to both repertoires.

At the end of bar 3 in the refrain of Gershwin's "A Foggy Day" (on "town") a special tetrachord makes its appearance, followed immediately by bass-note C, as shown in figure 24 at a).

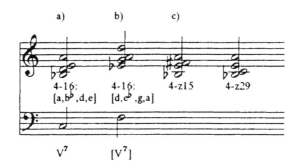

a)   b)   c)

4-16:   4-16:   4-z15   4-z29
[a,b♭,d,e]   [d,e♭,g,a]

V⁷   [V⁷]

Figure 24   George Gershwin

Later on, at the end of bar 25, a transposition of the same sonority occurs. In both instances the upper tetrachord is a form of 4-16 and part of an elaborate sonority of dominant function whose full figured-bass notation would be 9-7-6, a state-of-the art harmony in 1937 and one that has remained in the vocabulary of popular music and jazz.[26] Although in pitch structure it may resemble 4-z15 or 4-z29 superficially, as shown in figure 24 at c), it differs fundamentally from those sonorities with respect to interval content. Specifically, 4-16 contains no minor third or equivalent and it contains two perfect fourths (or their equivalents), the largest number for any tetrachord except for the ultra-diatonic "I Got Rhythm" tetrachord, 4-23. In Gershwin's voicing, which is perhaps most common in the popular repertoire, these two fourths (fifths) are grouped together at the top of the sonority, as D-A and E-A at a) in figure 24.

Returning for a moment to figure 21 at b) we can hear 4-16 as the upper tetrachord (f#-f-b♭-c) in the same sonority as 4-z15, the lower tetrachord; together they sum to trenchant pentad 5-30, which is a salient sonority in Berg's *Wozzeck*. In Arlen's "The Man That Got Away" (figure 21 at b) it sets the syllable "way" of "away," the final word in the song's title.

Both the major-seventh chord (4-20), discussed earlier, and 4-16 (for which we have no common name in tonal music) are heard prominently throughout Berg's *Wozzeck*. A particularly dramatic occurrence of both is shown in figure 25.

At bar 417 in Act I of *Wozzeck*, the harp begins an arpeggiation of a major-seventh chord on F (4-20). Six bars later (bar 423) with a change of only one note, from C to B, 4-20 mutates to become 4-16. The change in interval content is striking. The major-seventh chord has no tritone, whereas 4-16 does, and creation of this new interval is effected by the voice-leading motion from c^2 to b^1. At the same time, the number of major seconds changes from none to one, the number of minor thirds changes from one to none, and the number of major thirds reduces from two to one: a radical change in interval content through a change of only one note. This example highlights the fundamental importance of interval content in assaying the harmonic impact of sonorities, a basic musical factor of

4-20:   4-16:
[e,f,a,c] [e,f,a,b]

Figure 25   Alban Berg

which the American songwriters and their European predecessors were indubitably and profoundly aware.[27]

As is the case with many sonorities in the American popular idiom, the etymology of both 4-16 and 4-15 follows the path of the African-American blues. Remarkably, we also discover the blues thread in the next large category to be discussed, the octatonic.

V. The Octatonic Infusion

Another meeting ground of the European atonal and the American popular idioms is the octatonic harmony. The octatonic may be described briefly as a pitch system of large dimensions central to which is an eight-note scale, the octatonic scale.[28] This scale has three basic forms, one of which is c-d♭-e♭-e-f#-g-a-b♭. The other two forms are transpositions of this scale up one semitone and two semitones, respectively (Forte 1991a). Harmonies extracted from the scale are called octatonic harmonies. These may come from contiguous scalar components — for example, d#-e-f#-g — or they may be composed of scalar components that are not adjacent — for example, c#-e-g-c.

The provenance of the octatonic in European art music remains to be fully documented.[29] A similar situation obtains with respect to the presence of the octatonic in American popular music. Certainly, some of it, if not a great deal, has come down from the music of Debussy, but precisely how is not yet known; we do not know the lines of transmission, what music was involved, the extent of direct experience of Debussy's music by American songwriters, and so on.

On the other hand, all the American songwriters shared a common heritage of indigenous American popular music and, especially, music of African-Americans that had infused American popular music at least from the later nineteenth century. It is there that we might well look for traces of the octatonic. I suggest that the origin of the American octatonic is found in the African-American blues, a pervasive influence on American popular song.

Figure 26 The Octatonic

Specifically, as illustrated in figure 26 at a), the tonic triad plus the three blue notes gives the array c-e-g-e♭-g♭-b♭.[30] When these notes are arranged in ascending order it becomes evident that they occupy six of the eight positions in the octatonic scale. Thus, although the array is not coextensive with the ordered octatonic scale, it is an octatonic "collection" and corresponds to one of the six classes of hexachord within the total octatonic system of eight pitches.[31] It is not to the octatonic scale, but to the unordered octatonic collection that we refer, theoretically, when we hear instances of octatonic harmonies in American popular song, one of which I now cite (figure 27).

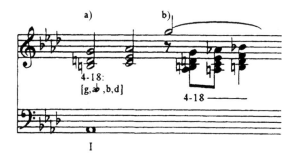

Figure 27   Richard Rodgers and Bill Evans

At a) in figure 27 is a schematic of the opening chords of the 1938 Rodgers and Hart song, "Spring Is Here." This consists of a dissonant harmony above bass A♭, the hallmark of the song, that resolves upward to the tonic triad. At b) in figure 27 is the beginning of the introduction to Bill Evans's recorded improvisation on this song (Evans 1959). Evans has taken the first sonority of the song and extended it in parallel motion, the upper voice of which follows the first three notes of an octatonic scalar pattern. In this way he intensifies the harmony, which, as indicated on the example, is octatonic tetrachord 4–18, one of the "classic" octatonic formations of European avant-garde octatonicism. An instance from that repertoire is cited in figure 28.

The whole-note chord in figure 28 is a form of 4-18, here serving in a cadential role in Stravinsky's *The Rite of Spring*, "Rival Tribes," at R58+1. In its full context (not shown) it completes an octatonic hexachord. As always, the orchestral voicing of the sonority is of interest since it projects or suppresses intervallic characteristics. Stravinsky has emphasized 4-18's single tritone E-B♭ by presenting it twice in the lower register, while, by contiguous placement, the major third (minor sixth) is emphasized at the expense of the two minor thirds of the harmony that comprise the diminished triad.

4-18
[e♭,e♮,g,b♭]

Figure 28   Igor Stravinsky

4-18
[f♯,g♮,a♯,c♯]

Figure 29   Claude Debussy

The excerpt from the beginning of Debussy's Prélude, "Feuilles mortes," shown in figure 29 contains 4-18 in the context of a 5-note octatonic sonority (5-31). Tetrachord 4-18 is notated separately on the lower staff, while the upper staff is given to an "F#^{7}" chord (4-27). Here, as in the Stravinsky example (figure 28) the composer chooses to deemphasize the primary octatonic intervallic characteristic, the diminished triad in the Stravinsky, and the full diminished seventh chord in the Debussy.

In "Feuilles mortes," as in many of Debussy's works, the key signature is enigmatic. Nevertheless, its presence illustrates the possibility that octatonic materials may surface within a composition that is essentially tonal in orientation, which is the case in the examples from American popular music that follow.

In this excerpt from Arlen's "Fun To Be Fooled" (figure 30) we hear a cadential progression to the tonic G-major triad cast in an intensified blues mode, with the blue seventh in the upper voice. Not only is the penultimate harmony octatonic (4-18), but together with the diminished triad that precedes it, we hear a complete octatonic hexachord. This hexachord, 6-z13, represents, coincidentally, one of the two classes of octatonic hexachord that occur as contiguous segments of the octatonic scale. Put

Figure 30   Harold Arlen

Figure 31   Cole Porter

another way, the cadential sonorities here may be regarded as verticals derived from the horizontal scalar form of the octatonic collection.

Near the end of Cole Porter's "I Concentrate On You," and setting the last occurrence of the keyword "concentrate," is the chromatic chord shown in figure 31. The upper tetrachord, octatonic 4-18, combined with the two notes on the lower staff, creates octatonic hexachord 6-27, a momentary and poignant excursion into the octatonic domain and one that is characteristic of many American popular songs.

In the next and antepenultimate illustration (figure 32) we hear two instances of octatonic infusion, with only slightly bluesy connotations, the first of which engenders a hexachord of type 6-27, as in the Porter example (figure 31).

The opening of the refrain of this famous song, Vernon Duke's "April In Paris," is shown at a) in figure 32. Its salient feature consists of the "F-minor triad" followed by the "B-major triad" on the upper staff. Combining the two harmonies produces octatonic hexachord 6-27.[32] A similarly striking octatonic moment occurs in the music that connects the bridge to the last section of the song, shown at b) in figure 32, where the

Figure 32 Vernon Duke

conflation of the mediant triad with added sixth and the dominant-seventh chord creates octatonic hexachord 6-z49.[33]

VI. *Critical Reception of the American Harmonies*

Another, and ironic, correspondence between European avant-garde music and the music of the American popular song lies in the area of critical reception. While the European music was often brutally savaged by critics as non-music, with the originally dismissive adjective "atonal," the harmonies of American popular music — often not distinguished from those of the emerging jazz idioms — were most often greeted by critics, both in the U.S. and abroad, with disdain. American songwriters, especially Gershwin by virtue of his status as a public figure, were exposed to the vitriolic opinions of major critics, such as those of Lawrence Gilman, dean of American newspaper music critics, in his *New York Tribune* review of Paul Whiteman's famous 1924 Whiteman Aeolian Hall concert, "An Experiment in Modern Music," which proved to be a provocative title. With regard to Gershwin's "Rhapsody in Blue" Gilman (1924) wrote: "one could weep over the lifelessness of its melody and harmony, so derivative, so stale, so inexpressive."[34]

Contemporary European avant-garde music and American popular song came together in Eva Gauthier's extraordinary concert, the "Recital of Ancient and Modern Music for Voice," also held in Aeolian Hall, on 1 November 1923, about three months before Whiteman's "Experiment."[35] In his review of the concert in *The New York Times*, H. C. Colles (1923) wrote: "Eclecticism in the making of a program is an excellent thing, and Miss Eva Gauthier was evidently determined to exploit its excellence to the full in the song recital which she gave last night at Aeolian Hall." He goes on to describe the plan of the program, which consisted of a first group, with Bellini arias and songs by Byrd and Purcell, and a second group, including Bartók's Hungarian Folk Songs, "the latest type of German 'Kunstlied' as shown in specimens by Paul Hindemith." Also included was "Lied der Waldtaube" from Schoenberg's "Gurrelieder" and songs by Darius Milhaud, Stravinsky's friend Maurice Delage, and Arthur Bliss. Colles then comes to the main feature of the concert:

Between them Miss Gauthier offered half a dozen ragtime songs straight from the vaudeville entertainments of Broadway, accompanied by Mr. George Gershwin, one of the ablest exponents of the craft, beginning with "Alexander's Ragtime Band" and ending with songs by Mr. Gershwin, continued by request of the audience until the singer had to confess that her repertory in this "lovely music" was exhausted. (Colles 1923)

Colles concludes: "...and so the thing was a failure." "It [ragtime and jazz] has developed into all it is capable of. It has become a thing which captivates people all over the world and hypnotizes them into dancing the night away: it is impossible to say why. But its home is not the concert room."

The "vaudeville entertainments" on the Gauthier concert were: Irving Berlin's "Alexander's Ragtime Band," Jerome Kern's "Siren's Song," Walter Donaldson's "Carolina in the Morning," Gershwin's "Swanee" and "I'll Build a Stairway to Paradise," and Gershwin's and Daly's "Innocent Ingenue Baby."[36] To be sure, these selections did not represent the best of American popular song as it would emerge in a few short years. Nevertheless, it is probably fair to say that Colles's opinion reflects the critics' generally negative view of American "vaudeville entertainments," a view heavily tinged by snobbism.

On the European side, the critical perspective on the new American popular genre was similarly percipient. Like Colles, Gilman, and other American critics, the Europeans did not distinguish between American popular song and jazz. As J. Bradford Robinson (1994) points out: "Early Weimar publicists regarded Berlin in particular as the quintessential jazz composer and the new style of American popular song in syncopated rhythms as a form of jazz." Robinson cites Adorno's pronouncement concerning the etiology of the harmonies of the American music, quoting Adorno as follows:

Nonenakkorde, Sixte ajoutée und andere Mixturen, wie der stereotype Blue Chord, parallele Verschiebung von Akkorden und was immer der Jazz an vertikalen Reizen zu bieten hat, is von Debussy entlehnt. (Wiesengrund-Adorno 1937)[37]

Adorno's opinion survives right up to the present time:

Since the elaborate structures of European art music are intimately related to its abundant harmonic resources, it follows that jazz has suffered a disadvantage in this area too. For many years, jazz relied not only on the structures of popular songs, but also on their relatively unsophisticated harmonies. As Hodeir points out, what passes for harmonic sophistication in the songs of Broadway and Tin Pan Alley is usually watered down from a European source, such as Debussy. (Bayles 1994; Hodier 1956)

One purpose of the present essay is to provide a fresher view of the expressive harmonies of the American popular song of the 1925–1950 period. These seem even more apt and affective when compared with their counterparts in European avant-garde music, and we can now see that etiolative efforts by critics over the years have been persistently turned back by natural developments in vernacular musics, particularly in jazz. Remarkably, some of the recent developments in that repertoire bring American popular music even closer to the seemingly remote European avant-garde atonal music of the early twentieth century, as I suggested at the beginning of this article. A final example illustrates.

Figure 33   Béla Bartók

This sonority, shown at a) in figure 33, occurs near the end of the tragically beautiful slow movement of Bartók's Fifth Quartet. Analysis reveals it to be a form of octatonic hexachord 6-z49. But it is also a sonority that might well be heard as a form of dominant seventh, a composite C# (D♭) seventh and G 7-6 sonority in a modern jazz setting for piano or big band, as shown at b) in figure 33, where the two tritone-related components interlock.

References

Bayles, Martha. 1994. *Hole in Our Soul: The Loss of Beauty and Meaning in American Popular Music.* New York: The Free Press.

Berg, Alban. 1971. *Alban Berg: Letters to His Wife.* Ed. and trans. Bernard Grun. London: Faber and Faber.

Berger, Arthur. 1963. "Problems of Pitch Organization in Stravinsky". *Perspectives of New Music* 2/1: 11–42.

Colles, H. C. 1923. "Review of a Recital by Eva Gauthier". *The New York Times* (2 November).

Evans, Bill. 1959. *Bill Evans Trio: Portrait in Jazz.* Berkeley: Riverside Records.

Forte, Allen. 1973. *The Structure of Atonal Music.* New Haven and London: Yale University Press.

Forte, Allen. 1991a. Debussy and the Octatonic. *Music Analysis* 10/1–2: 125–169.

Forte, Allen. 1991b. "The Mask of Tonality: Alban Berg's Symphonic Epilogue to *Wozzeck*", in David Gable and Robert P. Morgan, eds. *Alban Berg: Historical and Analytical Perspectives.* Oxford: Clarendon Press.

Forte, Allen. 1993. "Secrets of Melody: Line and Design in the Songs of Cole Porter". *The Musical Quarterly* 77/4: 607–647.

Forte, Allen. 1995. *The American Popular Ballad in the Golden Era 1924–1950.* Princeton: Princeton University Press.

Gilman, Lawrence. 1924. "Review of Paul Whiteman Orchestra Concert". *New York Tribune* (13 February).

Hodeir, André. 1956. *Jazz: Its Evolution and Essence.* New York: Grove Press.

Jablonski, Edward. 1987. *Gershwin.* New York: Doubleday.

McKenna, Dave. 1986. *Dancing In The Dark and Other Music Of Arthur Schwartz.* Concord: Concord Jazz, Inc.

Peterson, Oscar. 1959. *Oscar Peterson Plays the Cole Porter Songbook.* New York: Verve Records, Inc.

Robinson, J. Bradford. 1994. "The Jazz Essays of Theodor Adorno: Some Thoughts on Jazz Reception in Weimar Germany". *Popular Music* 13/1: 1–25.

Schoenberg, Arnold. 1911. *Harmonielehre.* Leipzig and Wien: Universal Edition.

Simms, Bryan. 1993. "The Theory of Pitch-Class Sets", in J. Dunsby, ed., *Models of Musical Analysis: Early Twentieth-Century Music.* Oxford: Blackwell Publishers.

Stein, Erwin. 1925. "Neue Formprinzipien", in *Von Neuer Musik: Beiträge zur Erkenntnis der neuzeitlichen Tonkunst.* Köln: F.J Marcan-Verlag.

Tatum, Art. 1991. In *You're the Top: Cole Porter in the 1930s.* Indiana Historical Society.

van den Toorn, Pieter. 1983. *The Music of Igor Stravinsky.* New Haven and London: Yale University Press.

Wiesengrund-Adorno, Theodor. 1937. *Zeitschrift für Sozialforschung*, 90.

Notes

1. "Harmonisch bedeutete das zunächst eine ungeheure Bereicherung. . . . Während die alte Harmonielehre nur wenige Dutzende von Akkorden . . . kannte, sind nunmehr alle Zusammenklänge, auch solche aus allen 12 Tönen möglich geworden" (Stein 1925, 60). For Schoenberg's own view of the new harmonies, see Schoenberg 1911, 435 ff.

2. Here at the outset I would like to emphasize that I regard the music of the European avant-garde as essentially atonal, or "non-tonal," if that is a more acceptable term, in the specific technical sense that a governing tonic-dominant triadic tonality is absent from the music of that repertoire. (At the same I time I am well aware that other kinds of "tonality" might be hypothesized as relevant to that music.) Thus, even when the relatives of the "tonal" chords of the American popular music occur in the European avant-garde music they do so as "strangers in paradise," in a totally different musical environment. This distinction underlies much of the discussion that is to follow, and therefore is of considerable importance to the discourse.

3. For names of pitch-class sets see Forte 1973. In this connection I wish to disclaim any didactic intention. The use of set names is only a convenience and does not imply an operative theory of harmony. Set names are particularly useful when the harmonies under consideration have no common names. In such cases the set names provide analytically neutral identifiers and are followed on the figures by a list of letter-names enclosed in brackets.

4. I do not intend to suggest that Bill Evans was a student of Webern's music! His harmonies are sometimes characterised as derivative from Debussy, which is debatable, to say the least, and suggests that writers on jazz often do not have discriminable hearing. But that there may be more explicit and "conscious" connections between jazz and avant-garde European music is certainly feasible; commentators have observed, for example, the influence of Bartók upon Chick Corea, in the latter's "Tweedle Dee."

5. Evans's chord is essentially a dominant harmony on D♭ whose root, typical of jazz practice, is missing (Evans 1959). In my discussion here, and throughout the present article, I take the published sheet-music of the American popular songs to be the authoritative texts, rather than the post-publication recordings, which is contrary to contemporary practice, in which the recorded music is the authentic text and the published score, if any, is often a corrupt representation of the music. See Forte 1993, 610.

6. Gershwin's role in the American idiom as innovative harmonist is perhaps most strikingly revealed in *The George Gershwin Songbook*, where he presented arrangements of eighteen of the songs he had composed between 1919 and 1932.

7. On yet another large topic, it is hoped that these correspondences will illuminate certain aspects of the history of tonality as it unfolded in the early twentieth century, with American popular music playing an important role. I am indebted to David Neumeyer for bringing this larger historical issue to my attention in a personal communication.

8. In his *Guide to Schoenberg's Gurrelieder* Alban Berg assigns this harmony thematic status. The origin of the chord as a distinct sonic entity is probably to be found in Wagnerian operas. For instance, it occurs in *Tristan und Isolde,* and elsewhere.

9. For a detailed discussion of the harmonic-motivic constituents of the opera, including the "major-seventh chord," see Forte 1991b.

10. Statements such as this concerning interval content derive from the tabular representation of tetrachords (and other sonorities) in Forte 1973.

11. In a remarkable way, the pentatonic chord with which the major-seventh chord alternates (ex. 3) further intensifies the interval of a perfect fifth. In fact, it intensifies it to

the maximum extent possible, for it is the only tetrachord that contains exactly three perfect fifths, the maximum number.

12. The major-seventh chord at the beginning of the refrain of "Night And Day" is some-times corrupted in jazz performances — even in Duke Ellington's famous rendition. On the other hand, Art Tatum (Tatum 1991) and Oscar Peterson (Peterson 1959) lavish considerable attention on it. Melodic statements of the major-seventh chord (4-20), although not abundant, are memorable. Among them, the incipits of Vernon Duke's "I Can't Get Started," Johnny Green's "I Wanna Be Loved," Jimmy Van Heusen's "I Thought About You," and bars 9 through 12 of George Gershwin's "A Foggy Day."

13. In his set of improvisations on "Dancing In The Dark," Dave McKenna (1986) empha-sizes the role of the major-seventh chord by announcing the opening phrase of the song as an unaccompanied melody, a very artistic touch.

14. In popular music and jazz as practiced now and in the past, the ubiquitous chord sym-bols superimposed above the upper staff, intended for players who could not negotiate the fully notated sheet music arrangements, obscure the total intervallic design of the harmony, which is basic to its aural profile. While adequate as mnemonic guides for improvisation, the chord symbols are completely unsuited to the formulation of ana-lytical interpretations.

15. The jazz origin explains the "nose-thumbing" gesture I mentioned at the outset, since, from the classical point of view, the chord was heard as a corruption of the simple triad through the intrusion of a lowbrow harmonic embellishment (the pentatonic sixth). With respect to "additions" (expository, that is), this is about as far as I care to go in a study of the psycho-sociology of the "chord of the added sixth."

16. See the discussion of "A Foggy Day" in Forte 1995.

17. The augmented triad, a fixture of earlier American popular music, might be regarded as the nucleus about which whole-tone sonorities developed, but its multiple occurrences in primarily "non-harmonic" passing-note contexts, often schmaltzy in effect, tend to blunt that hypothesis. Irving Berlin is the master of more elegant usage of that ultra-symmetric triad, as in bar two of the refrain of his "Blue Skies" (1927), where the descending passing note in the bass brings about its characteristic confluence of "major thirds."

18. The avant-garde music of Charles Ives often offers instances of this sonorous opposi-tion. Whole-tone as well as fourth chords and large diatonic sonorities are everywhere in his compositions. But as an American avant-garde composer he is excluded from the present study.

19. The occurrence of the "half-diminished-seventh" chord (4–27) here, while not totally unusual, is not representative of large-scale use of that sonority in the avant-garde rep-ertoire, excluding the many allusions to and quotations of the "Tristan chord." In the American popular-song repertoire, on the other hand, the half-diminished-seventh chord is a sonority of a very special kind, often reserved for moments of climactic quality.

20. In the larger context, however, these tonal implications vanish.

21. Pentad 5-30 is not, however, especially characteristic of Webern's music, but it is a staple item in Berg's harmonic vocabulary. In his *Wozzeck* it is associated throughout with the protagonist's underlying and often incoherent rage.

22. An instance of Schoenberg's initials A(rnold) Es = S(chönberg).

23. The "z" signifies that the tetrachord has a "twin" with the same interval content. Tetra-chords 4-z29 and 4-z15 are paired in this way.

24. The term was coined by David Lewin.

25. While 4-z29 contains one "triad," 4-z15 contains none. Like all other pairs of the "z" type, they are identical with respect to interval (dyadic) content, but their internal com-positions may differ considerably in terms of the subsets they contain.

26. By itself (without bass) the chord is found more often in jazz renditions than in popular song.

27. The question of direct connections between the European composers and the American songwriters remains open to some extent. But only Gershwin, as far as I know, was interested in modern "classical" music. Most of the songwriters were not even interested in traditional classical music, and some disliked it, for example, Irving Berlin. But Gershwin's interest was very lively and the Alban Berg-George Gershwin connection is interesting, although it probably does not have a direct bearing on this study. In Berg's letter to his wife dated 17 June 1928 (Berg 1971), he speaks of

> ...a very nice letter from Kolisch, who writes: "I don't know how often we have played the 'salon' arrangement" [Movements 2, 3, and 4 of Berg's *Lyric Suite*]. Mainly as a result of Gershwin's publicity. Gershwin has been fêted like a king in Paris, and he asked the Kolisch people to play my piece every day at the parties and receptions given in his honour. Next year America. [Rudolph Kolisch was Schoenberg's brother-in-law and leader of the Kolisch Quartet.]

Gershwin also attended the 1931 performance of Berg's Wozzeck in Philadelphia. He had spent time in Vienna, where on 3 May 1928, through Rudolf Kolisch, he met Berg, heard the Lyric Suite, played for him, and received an autographed excerpt from the Lyric Suite. See Jablonski 1987, 167. Jablonski also reports that Gershwin heard Berg's "string quartet" at the meeting, but this presumably was the *Lyric Suite* for String Quartet, not the earlier String Quartet, Op. 3.

28. The term octatonic was coined by Arthur Berger (1963).

29. But for an exhaustive study of the development of octatonicism in Stravinsky's music see van den Toorn 1983. See also Forte 1991a on Debussy's use of the octatonic.

30. It is important to understand that blue notes are not chromatically altered notes, although they are often loosely referred to in that way. The acculturation of blue notes occurred very early on in American popular music, so that they are full-fledged members of the pitch array and not dependent upon diatonic alteration for their *raison d'être*.

31. The hexachord shown in Example 21 belongs to class 6-z49, which is frequently found in Debussy's freely octatonic music (Forte 1991a). The ordered octatonic scale, as distinct from the unordered octatonic collection, is a late arrival in American popular music, entering via jazz practice where it was introduced as an "artificial" scale, known as the "diminished scale."

32. It is possible that Vernon Duke (né Vladimir Dukelsky) may have intuited the octatonic from his early experience with the well known Russian octatonic repertoire.

33. The occurrence of 6-z49 again here (see note 31) suggests a comment. In recent jazz, listeners often experience octatonic harmonies — although jazz players, not to mention critics, seem to be blissfully unaware of this association. For example, a "flat-ninth chord" (from bass up) a-g-c#-f#-b♭ is octatonic pentad 5-16. And if the "flat fifth" or "sharp fourth" is added, as it often is, the harmony is, as has already been pointed out, one of Debussy's favorite hexachords, 6-z49.

34. Gilman's opinion stands in stark contrast to Schoenberg's evaluation of Gershwin, written in 1938, shortly after Gershwin's death: "It seems to me beyond doubt that Gershwin was an innovator. What he has done with rhythm, harmony and melody is not merely style. It is fundamentally different from the mannerism of many a serious composer" (Schoenberg 1975, 476).

35. Eva Gauthier (1885–1958) was a very prominent singer, of French-Canadian provenance, whose speciality was innovative concerts.

36. Kern's "The Siren's Song," from *Leave it to Jane* (1917), is cast in his older style, heavily influenced by the English music hall and not representative of the newer trend in American musical comedy, heralded by Gershwin. Gershwin and William Daly collaborated on "Innocent Ingenue Baby" for the show *Our Nell*, which opened on 4 December 1922 and ran for 40 performances — not a successful endeavor.

37. "Ninth chords, the added sixth and other mixtures, such as the stereotypical blue chord, parallel shifting of chords and whatever jazz has to offer in vertical allurements is borrowed from Debussy." (my translation). As Robinson reminds us, jazz for Adorno was the music of fascism!

Contemporary Music Review
2000, Vol. 19, Part 1, pp. 37–62
Reprints available directly from the publisher
Photocopying permitted by license only

Performances in Early Hollywood Sound Films: Source Music, Background Music, and the Integrated Sound Track

David Neumeyer

Writing on film music, whether in the trade-book or academic literatures, has heavily favored symphonic background music over source music. Yet the more fundamental distinction made by industry professionals is between the image track and the sound track. Early in the history of sound film the integrated sound track became an artistic requirement for sound editors; this greater control also facilitated more crossover between musical styles. This essay problematizes the priority of symphonic background music in the early Hollywood cinema. I argue instead that priority should go to the integrated sound track, with all of its stylistic and narrative complexity. I demonstrate this by examining how song performances are placed in the sound track. Examples are drawn from the earliest sound feature films (1927–28), dramatic films and musicals from roughly 1932 to 1936, and *Casablanca* (1943).

KEYWORDS (1–6):   film theory, film music, *Casablanca*, diegetic, Max Steiner

Of the many genres in twentieth-century composition, music for cinema has proven to be one of the least amenable to theoretical modeling. To those familiar with the literature on the subject, this statement may seem paradoxical, since few notions in film theory are so widely accepted as the two principal constructs placing film music into a framework for interpretation: music serves a film's narrative system, and, therefore, the primary axis along which film music moves is determined by the implied physical space of the narrative world. Thus, music's "spatial anchoring"

(Metz [1975], 154) is either secure (source music) or undefined (background music or underscoring). Furthermore, since it is assumed in both film and film-music literatures that the primary repertoire of cinema is the narrative feature film (not documentaries, cartoons, or "abstract" films), the goal of film-music criticism or interpretation is to understand/read/analyze narrative functions, or music's role in shaping and furthering narrative processes. This is equally true whether one's orientation is that of a formalist or an ideological critic.

Despite such general agreement, film theory and film-music theory have not advanced at a comparable rate. First among reasons for this discrepancy must be the necessity for interdisciplinary work — that is, one needs to command film theory as well as historical and analytical music scholarship, an uncommon combination of skills. Among other reasons are the nature of cinema as a complex, multi-layered aesthetic object (and cultural artifact), the relative dearth of historical work linking music in cinema to stage practices, and the complexity of musical styles employed. The latter determined the "crossover" character of even early film music in a century when critics and scholars have tended to establish firm boundaries around what is "art music" and what is not, decisions regulated not only by social class and ethnic differences but also by the cultural politics of the absolute/program-music dichotomy, which originated in the mid-nineteenth century and whose arguments have, astonishingly, persisted nearly to the present day.

Difficulties notwithstanding, the politics of canonization for film music have been slowly proceeding in the trade-book literature and, during the past decade, in the academic literature as well. One of the most noticeable features of this process is that writers have continued to privilege symphonic background music strongly over source music. Claudia Gorbman's landmark study, for example, takes as its point of departure "the classical film score [within] the generalized paradigm of classical Hollywood film form of the thirties and forties"; this paradigmatic music is represented primarily by the symphonic scores of Max Steiner (Gorbman 1987, 7, 73). Katherine Kalinak argues more strenuously than does Gorbman for the equation of the visual and the aural as narrative controls in cinema (1992, 20–31), but she nevertheless maintains a sharp distinction between source music and the film score, at one point going so far as to assert that, since a substantial percentage of the earliest sound films were "restricted" to source music, "this meant that, in many films, there was no musical accompaniment at all" (67). She also describes the Hollywood score as "based on musical practices of the nineteenth century," although "other musical idioms, such as jazz and pop, found their way into the classical film score during the forties and fifties" (100, 102). Caryl Flinn, despite an explicit rejection of "rigid distinctions" between source and background music, and despite the fact that the two films which she reads closely (*Detour* and *Penny Serenade*) rely heavily on source music, nevertheless opens the first chapter of her book with the statement that "during the Hollywood studio era, film music was assigned a remarkably stable set of functions. It was ... used to enhance emotional moments in the story line, and to establish moods and maintain continuity between scenes. A similar uniformity was suggested by its style as well, since most scores were composed in a manner deeply influenced by ... Wagner and Richard Strauss" (Flinn 1992, 11, 13). Finally, the association between source music and the performances that dominate musicals leads Royal S. Brown to assert matter of factly that the symphonic background score "has become a permanent fixture of commercial cinema," and, therefore, "this type of music ... will serve as the principal object of discussion [here]. Song scores for film musicals such as *Singin' in the Rain*, on the other hand, fall outside the scope of this study" (1994, 22).

To a certain extent, the authors cited above are merely following the historical biases of the film industry itself. By 1935, the integrated sound track with effective post-production sound mixing was in place, and the first Academy Award for an original dramatic score was presented to Max Steiner for his music to John Ford's *The Informer*.[1] By this time, also, film credits for music were divided between the composer of the background music ("Music by ... "), the composer and lyricist for any songs especially written for the film ("'[Song title]' by [lyricist] & [composer]"), the conductor (if not the background-score composer or music director), and the studio music department head ("music director"), whether or not the latter had an active role in the production. By about 1940, the orchestrator of the background score often received a credit, too. Typically, the background-score composer did not do dance-band or song arrangements; for example, in *Casablanca* (1943), Max Steiner wrote the background score but Frank Perkins did the song arrangements. Of course, the career path followed by Steiner himself — from "arranger" to "orchestrator" to "composer" — did remain available, an industry structure still in place today, decades after the dissolution of the old studio music departments.

The "composer," then, had a privileged status in the Hollywood studio music department. The class differences were expressed succinctly by MGM's music director Herbert Stothart: "The development of new song writers is of relatively small importance. The important thing that the screen is doing to-day is in giving opportunities to composers, who, imbued with fresh vision, are carrying on the work started by men like Stravinsky, and applying its modern impressionistic principles to the drama of the screen" (1938, 139). The most successful composers received an intertitle to themselves in the film's main-title sequence, usually just before the director and producer (this solo billing was part of Steiner's contract when he moved from RKO to Warners in 1936). Nevertheless, despite a long history of attempts to merge high art and the cinema — starting with Saint-Saëns' score for *L'Assassinat du Duc de Guise* (1908) and the Pathé and Edison Companies' filming of opera scenes after 1910 (Altman 1992c, 116), through similar efforts by Warners with Vitaphone shorts in the mid-1920s, to Warners' importation of Erich Wolfgang Korngold in 1935, Stravinsky and Schoenberg's abortive negotiations with MGM about the same time (Rosar 1989), several "opera-musicals" in the mid-to-late-thirties, and finally Disney's *Fantasia* (1940) — film composers in the United States never achieved the same status as their colleagues who wrote for the concert stage or opera (Palmer 1990, 9). Despite professional education that was the same in most instances, concert composers were able to command respect that film composers who ventured into writing concert works found almost impossible to gain for themselves (especially after 1950), the most notable examples being Franz Waxman and Bernard Herrmann. Others who had been accepted as concert composers, especially Korngold and Miklos Rozsa, sullied their reputations by subsequently working for the film industry (Thomas 1991, 82–83).

The complex set of issues related to the status of Hollywood film composers — and the sharp differences between America and Europe in that respect — could be the subject of an extended socio-cultural study.[2] I am concerned here with just one aspect of the problem: how the bias toward "classical" music, and therefore toward the symphonic background score, has influenced — and in my view distorted — our interpretative practices with respect to music's role in the feature film, and therefore our understandings of the origins and character of the sound cinema in Hollywood. The strategy is to problematize the idea of symphonic music's priority by problematizing the source music/background music dichotomy. I will argue instead that precedence in the historical and critical study of music in cinema should go to the integrated sound track, with all of its stylistic and narrative complexity. This move will permit us to disentangle the components of the binary pair symphonic-background/popular-source and to recognize this particular disposition of terms as only one possibility among several. The section below advances some further historical preliminaries, making reference mainly to films between 1927 and 1935. Thereafter, I develop a theoretical model which reinterprets a simple hierarchy crowned by the source/background pair as a field or network where this pair is one item. Close reading of sequences from *Casablanca* will provide examples of application. The goal of this essay, then, is to articulate a few elements of a critical attitude which specifically accounts for the source-music/background-music dichotomy but at the same time moves past it toward a more complex and more comprehensive set of categories for music in the sound cinema. With such categories in place, we may eventually be able to integrate music in a completely satisfying way into historical or critical studies of the sound track.

Although source/background continues to be regarded as a basic category for the study of film music, the more fundamental distinction made by industry professionals is between the image track and the sound track. Early on in the history of sound film, the integrated sound track became an artistic requirement for sound editors, and musicians as a result were able to exploit various kinds of ambiguity in "spatial anchoring," Christian Metz's term for the degree to which a recorded sound is "attached" to its object — in effect a measure of its "diegetic-ness" or its "realism." Although film-genre differences were recognized (as components of both production and marketing), the basic techniques of sound design, including music's integration into it, were the same regardless of genre. This fact suggests what I believe the historical record plainly shows: that it was possible for directors and sound designers creatively to confuse the boundaries of genre by, for example, emphasizing performances in dramatic films — as in *Grand Hotel* (1932) or *The Informer* (1935), for instance — or by including extensive background music, as often happens even in early musicals (e.g., *Love Me Tonight* [1932] or *Naughty Marietta* [1935]).

Although the terms "background" (or "underscoring") and "source" are routinely used — and their definitions well understood — in film music composition and criticism today (Handzo 1985, 408), they are *not* coextensive with the categories used in many Hollywood studio cue sheets of the thirties and forties: "visual vocal" or "visual instrumental" and "background vocal" or "background instrumental."[3] In the current definition, "source music" refers to music which seems to emanate from the world of the film's narrative, such as a song performance by an actor, music played at an onscreen concert, or offscreen whistling or humming associated with a character or an assumed physical space, such as a room we can only glimpse through a partly open door. Background music cannot be similarly located in the narrative world but instead hovers in an ambiguous intermediate "space" between film and audience similar to that occupied by voice-over narration. Claudia Gorbman's terms "diegetic" and "non-diegetic," which are now generally accepted by scholars, mean the same as "source" and "background" music, respectively (1987, 3). The cue-sheet terms "visual vocal" and "visual instrumental," on the other hand, refer to *onscreen* source music only, while "background vocal" and "background instrumental" may refer to offscreen source music or to underscoring. The reasons for these distinctions were production-related: onscreen performances generally commanded higher copyright permissions fees than did background uses. For example, when Warners' music director, Leo Forbstein, negotiated for the use of "Old Man Mose" in *Casablanca*, the rates he was quoted by the New York office were $350 for background instrumental use, $500 for background vocal, $750 for visual instrumental, and $1000 for visual vocal.[4]

The discontinuity between critical definitions and practice is crucial, because it undercuts a linked set of binary oppositions. If non-diegetic music is opposed to diegetic — that is, background to source — then a symphonic sound is opposed to the dance band, "classical" music to popular (jazz, or later, rock), and, therefore, high art and aesthetic values are set against low art and commercial value. (This is a statistical claim: of course, it is possible to have symphonic music as source music, but in American movies of the period it is far more likely that source music will be played by a dance band or theater orchestra.)[5] Symphonic background music can make a case for an educative function, in that it encourages appreciation of the historical monuments of European culture, and it promotes moral training (by refining control of emotions, an important role for music in middle-class society since the early nineteenth century). Popular source music, on the other hand, is at best harmless and superficial entertainment, at worst degenerate, especially in its association with dance halls, private clubs, and bars, and in its emphasis on sexual and illicit behavior.[6]

But if the diegetic/non-diegetic dichotomy breaks down in practice, then it cannot be said unequivocally that classical Hollywood sound film supports the table of oppositions just described above. If the theatrical and cinematic roots of background scoring were stylistically mixed, it cannot be reasonably maintained that symphonic background scoring somehow upholds superior aesthetic values while source music succumbs to the degraded or superficial. And, if so, it cannot also be reasonably maintained that the dramatic feature film (which has relied most heavily on underscoring) should be privileged over the film musical. In other words, even if it is statistically true that in feature films of the thirties and forties symphonic music predominates in the background and popular music prevails onscreen, this does not mean that the distinction between source and background must necessarily be tied to simplistic dichotomies of musical styles, narrative functions, or hierarchies of value.

A brief survey of the antecedents of the classical Hollywood sound film readily reveals a much more complex practice. In the silent era, the musical performances that accompanied films routinely mixed musical styles, sometimes in jarring fashion, even in prestige productions:

The action [in *The Rose of the World* (Paramount 1918)] is set in British imperial India, and [the prepared score provides] an original love theme and a Hindu motif, . . . interwoven with popular melodies and light classics. . . . The audience heard Massenet's *Élegie*, "Somewhere a Voice is Calling," "Home, Sweet Home," two different segments of the *William Tell Overture*, Nevin's "The Rosary," and, accompanying scenes of the return to England, "Sailor Beware!" (Koszarski 1990, 47)

Small-town pianists or organists playing matinees and relying on published collections such as Erno Rapée's *Motion Picture Moods* ([1924]) could switch almost instantly from a Chopin prelude to George Root's "Tramp, Tramp, Tramp," or from the last movement of Beethoven's "Moonlight" Sonata to *Agitato No. 3* by "photoplay" composer Otto Langey. The pragmatic authors of technical manuals for silent-film accompaniment recognized the need for this stylistic diversity: for example, in one manual, aspiring performers are advised to "visit the music shops, whenever you have an opportunity, and look over the novelties in popular music as well as in the better class of publications" (Lang and West, [1920], 62). Having found and purchased a variety of suitable musics, one then must "use wisdom in combining 'lighter stuff' and artistic material, work[ing] gradually towards a happy union of the two, with music of real worth predominating." In another manual, we find that "one or two enterprising firms have gone out of their way to cater for the cinema organist by publishing music of a popular nature that is particularly useful in the cinema" (Tootell 1927, 55). Compositions by "outstanding composers," such as Jan Hurst ('Melodie d'Amour') and J. Stuart Archer ('Intermezzo') "cannot be too highly recommended."

The symphonic background score for sound film derives principally from the silent-film orchestral performances that were possible in larger theaters in cities and "recorded for posterity" in the earliest sound-synchronized feature films, Warner Brothers' *Don Juan* (1926) and *The Jazz Singer* (1927). Even near the beginning of Louis Singer's partly original, partly compiled background score for *The Jazz Singer*, we hear the love theme from Tchaikovsky's "Romeo and Juliet" Overture (which Singer uses "to represent Jack Robin's feelings for his parents") followed by "East Side, West Side" for establishing shots of a New York neighborhood (Kalinak 1992, 68). It is true that the symphonic accompaniment is set in sharp relief against Al Jolson's famous song performances (no leitmotifs from the latter invade the background music), but the strongest juxtaposition in the film involves diegetic music: the extended New York synagogue scene, which features cantor Joseph Rosenblatt's performance, and the immediately following Paris café-restaurant scene in which Jolson sings his first numbers: "Dirty Hands, Dirty Face" and "Toot, Toot, Tootsie, Goodbye." (I am discounting an earlier number supposed to be by the immature Jack Robin [Jakie Rabinowitz]. That performance simply does not have the effect of the later scene, in which Jolson himself first appears as the adult Robin [Geduld 1975, 182].) Because of Jolson's song performances and despite its continuous underscoring, *The Jazz Singer* is generally regarded as a musical, not a dramatic feature. In a final irony, before 1932, when post-production re-recording was first generally used, background music was more likely to be employed in a musical than in a dramatic feature: "In *The Love Parade* (1929), for instance, diegetic music in the production numbers spills over as nondiegetic music for ensuing scenes" (Kalinak 1992, 68).

Cinema music's tradition of stylistic variety and its fluid movement between the diegetic and non-diegetic tend to break down the status of the latter pair as the principal category for film-music interpretation. The linkage of the non-diegetic to the symphonic, and thus (potentially) to classical high art was culturally imposed, and certainly not intrinsic to any demands of cinematic technology or any generalizable demands of narrative or production style. Nor, as we have seen, was symphonic music stylistically monolithic: classical high art (by which we mean above all Beethoven) or imitations of the style of classical high art were relatively uncommon even in the silent era; the traditional orchestra was used as often for the "light classics" of French and Italian theatrical styles, Viennese operetta, and Broadway shows, as it was for that *lingua franca* of underscoring, the Wagner/Strauss symphonic-operatic style. The popular song style found its way into underscoring, as in the jazz melody Steiner wrote for the female lead in *The Informer* (1935) or the background cues for *Shall We Dance* (1937), based on original songs Gershwin wrote for this Astaire-Rogers vehicle (Mueller 1985, 115). In the forties, the interplay between the symphonic and popular styles increased (as in *Casablanca* or, spectacularly, in *Laura* [1944]). Later still, Alex North built a symphonic score on jazz styles (*A Streetcar Named Desire* [1951]), Duke Ellington wrote an entire background score for a small jazz ensemble (*Anatomy of a Murder* [1959]), rock and roll background scores became fashionable, and finally in the eighties "crossover" scores became the norm.

At this point, some qualification of an earlier comment is in order. The situation in film-music criticism is not quite so stark as I have portrayed it above. Gorbman, for example, does allow music a remarkable range of action even as she maintains the binary opposition diegetic/non-diegetic as a basic theoretical construct:

the only element of filmic discourse that appears extensively in non-diegetic as well as diegetic contexts, and often freely crosses in between, is music. Once we understand the flexibility that music enjoys with respect to the film's diegesis, we begin to recognize how many different kinds of functions it can have: temporal, spatial, dramatic, structural, denotative, connotative — both within the diachronic flow of a film and at various interpretive levels simultaneously (1987, 22).

It is exactly this flexibility, however, which finally grants priority to non-diegetic music. For, although it might seem that diegetic music would have the advantage (as it is more closely tied to the film's narrative, which music — like all sound-track elements — must serve), it is in fact that very closeness which inhibits diegetic music's range of functions, its ability to "inflect the narrative with emotive values" (4). Performances delay, and sometimes disrupt, the flow of narrative, as they require that we pay attention to them in order to recognize and appreciate them as artistic events — that is, as musical performances in the usual sense. Special care must be taken to motivate a performance if it is to seem realistic (that is, relevant to the plot); beginnings and endings in particular must be managed in a natural fashion. The lyrics — and the song title itself — are situated uncertainly in the sound track, somewhere between music and dialogue. The title or text may be relevant to the narrative or they may not; to discover which is the case, once again, requires some attention on the part of the film spectator.

Non-diegetic music, on the other hand, may more readily subordinate itself to the image track and act as an almost subliminal influence on the viewer (hence the "unheard melodies" of Gorbman's title). Indeed, specific genres of composition were developed to facilitate this in the early sound-film era by Max Steiner and others (Neumeyer 1995). Their models were drawn from the musical stage, including opera, operetta, and melodrama. By 1935, most of the familiar and characteristic practices of background scoring for cinema were already in place.

Thus, we have not really advanced beyond the critical framework in which background music primarily serves to reinforce the cinematic illusion, and source music primarily entertains with the occasional formal performance. All other attributes are reduced to qualifiers of the source/ background or diegetic/non-diegetic pair. As an illustration, I cite the first performance in *Casablanca*: Dooley Wilson singing and playing "It Had to Be You." The music begins offscreen during a shot of the neon sign atop the front door of Rick's *Café americaine*; it continues through a cut inside and a moderately slow pan across the café to a full shot of Wilson (spotlighted) at his piano singing and playing the song's final phrase. The dynamic (or sound) level is constant throughout, and yet we are inclined to regard the cue as diegetic because the performance is continuous before Wilson appears onscreen. Even if we accept Gorbman's flexible boundaries between the diegetic and non-diegetic, it is only possible to read the cue as a journey from the non-diegetic to the diegetic, though there must be lingering doubt about the former because of violation of the convention that non-diegetic music is instrumental. What we cannot do is understand the unrealistic sound level as the deciding agent in hearing the music (even though those levels are problematic both for the establishing shot of the sign and for Wilson's onscreen shot [assuming that the camera represents the position of the viewer/auditor]). At best the discrepancies "muddy" the realism of the performance.

To counter the enforced priorities of such readings as the one I have just constructed, I propose a more elaborate theoretical model which displaces the diegetic/non-diegetic pair as the primary category for film-music analysis and establishes instead a field or network of several interacting binary pairs (see figure 1). The strategy exemplified by this model is to break apart diegetic and non-diegetic from their several qualifiers and then to assume that any of the categories or oppositions thus defined may direct interpretation of music's functions in a sequence or scene.

1. Diegetic/non-diegetic (or source/background).
2. Onscreen/offscreen.
3. Vocal/instrumental: performance forces.
4. Rerecording: synchronized/not-synchronized.
5. Sound Levels: "Realistic"/unrealistic (for diegetic music); loud/soft (for non-diegetic music).
6. Musically continuous/discontinuous.
7. Musically closed/open.
8. Formal interaction of cutting and music: yes/no.
9. Motivation, or narrative plausibility: yes/no.
10. "Pure"/culturally or cinematically coded.

Figure 1   Binary Pairs for film-music analysis

The first pair in figure 1, diegetic/non-diegetic (or source/background), refers narrowly to spatial anchoring, or plausibility in the physical world represented in the image track. "Non-diegetic" may or may not include point-of-view music associated with a character's subjectivity, since such music can only be located indirectly at best, that is, "in the mind." Bordwell and Thompson label point-of-view sound "internal diegetic" (1990, 254).

The second opposition is onscreen/offscreen, which refers narrowly to what the camera frames at the time the music sounds. Although the notion may be difficult to grasp, it is possible to have onscreen non-diegetic music if a song is not a "public" performance but an expression of the singer's subjectivity; under such circumstances it is plausible that the singer does not know that he or she is performing. Abbate (1991, xii) argues that this is the typical state of nineteenth-century opera (see also Buhler and Neumeyer 1994, 377–381).

The next pair is straightforward: performance forces, vocal or instrumental. Unless further refinement is needed for a specific reading, the term "vocal" will also enclose voice with instrumental accompaniment.

Rerecording is characterized as synchronized or not-synchronized. This refers narrowly to the degree to which synchronization or, more likely, the lack of such coordination, becomes a noticeable feature of a shot or sequence. "Non-sychronized" non-diegetic cues are included under "Formal interaction of cutting and music" below.

The next category is sound levels, which encloses terms such as "dynamic levels," "mixing levels", or "loudness." For diegetic music, sound levels may be called realistic/unrealistic; for non-diegetic music, the basic opposition is loud/soft, with extremes considered to be "excessively loud" (music that forces itself strongly on the spectator's attention, such as a sudden swell under end credits) or "excessively soft" (music dubbed so quietly that its affect is indistinct or its leitmotivic references inaudible). These continua function within limits established by technology, namely, microphones and theater sound systems (Handzo 1985, 393–404, 417–418) and by studio sound design practices (Altman 1992b). Sound levels are perhaps the most likely sound-track elements to undermine the diegetic/non-diegetic, for they continually raise the question of sound/image scale-matching or auditory perspective (Altman 1992b, 56, 49): Are sounds "appropriate" to the depicted physical space and distance from the camera? The mismatch between image scale and sound scale is a defining feature of sound design after the mid-thirties (Altman 1992b, 54).

The next two pairs are concerned closely with musical phenomena. Musically continuous/discontinuous refers to traditional musical continuity of phrase, harmonic and melodic development, etc. Musically closed/open refers to the "cadence" and related devices of musical closure, including those created by completing conventional musical-form schemata.

Formal interaction of cutting and music can be characterized as either being present or absent: yes/no. Such design parallelisms between shot sequences and musical phrasing or expressive articulations may apply at a local level (for example, repeated mickey-mousing or phrases matched to shots) or at a larger level, as when a single shot used for an entire performance, with cutting matched to phrasing throughout, or when a cue covers a specific sequence or scene. Melodramatic cues always interact locally with the image track; "non-sychronized," "contrapuntal," or "mood" cues do not interact at a local level, and may or may not interact at a larger level.[7]

Motivation for music, or its narrative plausibility, may be supplied by a number of means. A character may be a musician (such as Leslie Howard in *Intermezzo* or Dooley Wilson in *Casablanca*), or may experience a sudden shock (as in Rick's response to seeing Ilsa in *Casablanca*). Dialogue readily supplies motivation ("Hear the music"; "Do you remember that song we used to sing?"; "Play some of the old songs"), as does the image track (an orchestra, dance band, radio, or phonograph in the background of a shot). Whether mickey-mousing is motivated by the image track is open to question.

The final category might be regarded as a contextual scale. Its terms (after Gorbman 1987, 12–13) are "pure" and either "culturally or cinematically coded." The pure performance is autonomous, as close to a concert as possible, in the sense that listening to the design, structure, and affect of the music itself is of primary importance (this is possible only in a filmed concert performance, preferably without any film editing, but the pure performance may be approached in main title cues, in the extended end credit cues of contemporary films, or even in unmotivated song performances). Music that is coded is necessarily contextual, whether the cultural musical code of "Scottish music" or the cinematic musical code of a leitmotif used for a particular character. Genre conventions may also be included here (e.g., a montage sequence will have background music, a chase scene needs a "hurry" cue, etc.).

As the description of the last pair suggests, it is often useful to think of the binary terms in figure 1 not as absolute categories but as endpoints on a continuum. For example, point-of-view music may be regarded as midway between diegetic and non-diegetic, combining properties of both. The same is true of music that is apparently diegetic but placed in an unstable or uncertain physical environment (as in a dream). The "off/on" alternatives for musical closure might be construed, instead, as a series of levels extending from the conventional final cadence of a clearly defined musical form, to clear cadential closure but on an intermediate phrase, to a fade-out managed by the sound editor, to an abrupt mid-phrase cutoff. And so on for other pairs in the list.

To demonstrate how this model might be applied, I have chosen an extended example from *Casablanca*, a fifteen-minute segment which covers the second half of the thirty-minute café scene near the beginning of the picture. Figure 2 provides a time-line summary of this segment, which covers the period from Major Strasser's first entrance into the café to Ilsa and Laszlo's exit some time later the same evening. Each of the five sequences is organized around a musical performance. In sequence 1, Sam and the band play offscreen a version of "I'm Just Wild About Harry." In the second sequence, they perform mostly offscreen "Heaven Can Wait." The third sequence parallels the second in that the performance begins onscreen then moves off; Sam plays a medley consisting of "Speak to Me of Love" and "Love for Sale." Sequence 4 introduces a featured performer, Corinna Mura, playing and singing *Tango delle Rose*. The final sequence begins with Ilsa's requests of Sam and passes into one of the most famous symphonic cues in cinema, Steiner's development of "As Time Goes By."

The first sequence begins shortly before Major Strasser's appearance in the café and ends with the arrest of Ugarte. The band's performance of "I'm Just Wild About Harry" is entirely offscreen, but we readily accept it as diegetic because of previous highlighted performances (including "Knock on Wood" and "Shine"). Nevertheless, the diegetic status is undercut by an unmotivated drop-out in the middle of the scene: the music

Sequence 1:

0:00   Music in as Major Strasser enters the café . ("I'm Just Wild About Harry")
2:30   (approx.) Music out under gun shots

Sequence 2:

3:05   Music in after Rick directs Sam to start playing again
        (We see the orchestra and Sam briefly.) ("Heaven Can Wait")

Sequence 3:

5:37   Laszlo and Ilsa enter the café
        (They pass by Sam on their way to a table. A subsequent medium shot of
        Sam at his piano shows him looking over his shoulder towards them.)
        ("Speak to Me of Love"; then "Love for Sale")
7:20   Music out as Strasser comes to their table

Sequence 4:

8:17   *Tango delle Rose* performance
        (Singer with guitar, begins onscreen, goes offscreen twice, then finishes
        onscreen.)
10:05   Performance finished

Sequence 5:

10:10   Ilsa asks the waiter to send Sam to her table
10:34   Sam appears with his piano
10:53   He plays, ("Avalon")
11:25   stops
11:49   She hums "As Time Goes By"
11:56   He plays,
12:04   sings,
12:48   stops
12:51   Cue 4,7 begins with the stinger chord.
15:26   Cue 4,7 out

Figure 2   A segment from *Casablanca* (beginning at approximately 20:30)

simply disappears for several moments while Ugarte is talking in the
casino room. If the diegetic must be "realistic" — and how can we be convinced that the actors can hear it otherwise? — then any weaknesses in
the cinematic illusion of a musical reality, so to speak, undercut the
notion of the "diegetic." Unless we are simply talking about an editing
error, which seems unlikely, it would seem that our standards for "realism" in dialogue (or diegetic speech) are higher than they are for diegetic
music.

The performance, then, is uncertainly diegetic, offscreen, instrumental, with a generally realistic sound level (Captain Renault and Rick are talking in the latter's office; the music comes in as the office door is opened from the outside; sound comes up plausibly with the cut to the café, although it then goes under dialogue noticeably). The performance is musically discontinuous because of the unmotivated drop-out, and it is also musically open (it is unclear if we hear the ending of the song as the music goes out under gun shots). Both characteristics are unusual but by no means unknown in diegetic performances.

Film editing and musical design interact: the pianist plays the verse, then the orchestra plays the chorus, the articulation happening as Renault greets Strasser. Nor is there any ambiguity about motivation: the café performance starts when the musicians are ready; it goes out with the disturbance of Ugarte's arrest (as if the musicians are disconcerted, too, by the gunfire). Whether the performance leans more toward the pure or coded is unclear, but this is a typical problem with non-featured performances, which combine the cultural musical code — café dance band playing popular music — with the role of "disengaged" background music, that is, music that interacts so little with the image track that it could be listened to separately and autonomously.

The association of the song "I'm Just Wild About Harry" with Major Strasser is obviously ironic (and thus less believable as diegetic), since this rather enthusiastic love song is hardly appropriate for the unloved, unloving, and unloveable villain. Such links between song titles and action in the environment of the performance ought to occur at random, and certainly with nothing like the persistent regularity that it happens in the movies (particularly this one). One might best place such associations under a larger level of editing and musical design: the song performance is placed "by design" at this point rather than some other, equally good spot because of the association, its only motivation. (The motivation is not so strong as it might be, of course, because the film makers cannot be sure how many in the audience will know the song and therefore catch the allusion.)

One might readily argue, then, that the diegetic status of the music is a secondary factor in this sequence, because the performance is partly treated as it would be were it "properly" nondiegetic. More important are the linking of the song title with Strasser, the formal interaction of cutting and musical form, and even the lack of musical continuity and closure.

The second sequence follows Ugarte's arrest, beginning as the band's set resumes; the song is "Heaven Can Wait," which continues through the brief interrogation of Rick by Strasser as they sit at a table with Renault. The performance is plainly diegetic; the performers are onscreen to begin, then move offscreen for the remainder. Yet the diegetic is undercut by a lack of synchronization (Sam's hands) and a jump cut that affects the music at the beginning, slicing off some notes and inserting an audible pop as we jump from Sam to the orchestra (this clumsy transition is apparently due to last-minute editing that deleted a performance of "Dat's What Noah Done" [Lebo 1992, 181]). The title association undercuts the diegetic, as well: Heaven (escape from Casablanca) can wait after Ugarte is arrested and Rick is interviewed by Strasser. (It should also be pointed out that the piano heard on the sound track, here and elsewhere in the film, is obviously not an instrument like the white-painted upright we see onscreen.)

As in sequence 1, the dynamic level is generally realistic but goes under dialogue noticeably. The initial diegetic status is presented in an exaggerated way; motivated by Rick's direction that the band resume playing, the performance begins in an unnaturally short amount of time at a sound level that is noticeably loud. Synchronization with Sam's hands and voice is poor. The performance is musically continuous, but open (only because the ending fades out under dialogue). The balance between the pure and the coded is, likewise, similar to sequence 1.

Thus, "Heaven Can Wait" begins — awkwardly — as diegetic music but then wanders into the same quasi-background "limbo" as "I'm Just Wild About Harry," a condition in which the song-title association is probably more important than spatial anchoring.

The third sequence is very much like the second. The music begins simultaneously with the entrance of Ilsa and Laszlo into the café; it goes out as Strasser approaches their table. Note the inappropriate sound levels at the beginning; based on what we have heard previously, Sam should be a considerable distance away, at the back of the building, not a mere fifteen feet, as we discover when Ilsa and Laszlo advance into the café and walk by him.

The performance is thus (awkwardly) diegetic, briefly onscreen, then off, with a generally realistic sound level (except for the opening, although the level throughout lacks sufficient change to match character movement about the café or differing shot distances). The music is designed in the recognizable form of a medley but the ending is open and unmotivated: the music simply goes out when Strasser appears. Editing and musical design interact to the extent that the performance begins almost simultaneously with the entrance of Ilsa and Laszlo.

The performance of these songs is once again motivated by title associations ("Speak to Me of Love" on Ilsa's entrance; "Love for Sale" as Laszlo and Berger talk about the ring). In preparation for the next sequence, Ilsa mentions Sam to the waiter. The same balance between pure and coded performance is maintained as in previous sequences, but the use of romantic ballads presages the strong cinematic coding connecting "As Time Goes By" with Ilsa and Rick's affair in Paris.

In the fourth sequence, Corinna Mura's performance of *Tango delle Rose* is plausibly motivated; she is a featured soloist in the café performing a music that is set apart stylistically from anything heard heretofore (traditional Spanish, although the text is sung in French). Her performance is framed by audience applause, which we have not heard since the "Knock on Wood"/"Shine" set early in the café segment. The performance also stands out from the preceding three sequences because it is vocal with instrumental accompaniment. The music is diegetic, of course, with a fairly regular patterning of on/off/on/off/onscreen, which contributes to undercutting the diegetic status because the dynamics are unrealistic; the singing voice goes under dialogue unnaturally during each offscreen sequence. The cue is musically continuous and closed, and editing and musical design interact — after the short verse onscreen, the chorus goes offscreen — but since this happens twice the effect is too obviously patterned. In addition, the performance is unrealistically telescoped; it is supposed to be a complete featured number, experienced in clock time, but it actually lasts less then two minutes.

As it turns out, then, this sequence has more in common with the previous three than might have been expected. The balance should have shifted strongly in favor of a pure performance: unlike the situation created by previous cues, the viewer is alerted by the spotlighted entrance and the audience applause to regard this as a featured performance, the performer has had no previous character role in the film, and neither the song's title nor its style has any obvious association with the narrative. Nevertheless, the effect of a pure performance is sabotaged by the intercutting and dialogue. One can readily imagine that Corinna Mura, who was under contract to Warners, was not pleased with the studio's treatment of her only number in this film, but the rapid pace of cutting and plot is consistent with the Warner Bros. studio style (Bordwell, Staiger, and Thompson 1985, 62; Harmetz 1992, 259, 261; Miller 1992, 58).[8]

Sequence five contains some of the film's most famous moments. The music includes an aborted instrumental performance of "Avalon," followed by "As Time Goes By" (piano, then voice), and a symphonic background cue that continues to the end of the scene (the first symphonic music heard since the main titles and opening scene). This sequence includes the most realistic diegetic music so far (even Sam's hands are better synchronized with the sound track). After Sam pushes the piano over to Ilsa's table, his "private performance" of "As Time Goes By" is interrupted by Rick. A stinger chord catches Rick's surprise, and "As Time Goes By" promptly moves into the underscoring. The level of motivation for this background cue is very high: the chord itself is as much sound effect — a sharply drawn-in breath — as it is music: we "hear" the air vibrating with the shock of this reunion. The oboe's subsequent, languid rendering of the tune over this mildly dissonant chord is a musical equivalent of the characters' slowly evolving subjective state, and thus it is questionable whether this music is really background music at all (that is to say, it has the characteristic problem of point-of-view music, which is readily understood as a musical "translation" of what the actors are feeling, a window on their subjectivity). From that point on, the music is a typical Steiner melodramatic cue, so closely tied to the screen action that the result is very close to voice-over narration: "As Time Goes By" is converted to a waltz affect (but with tonally vague half-diminished seventh chords) when Paris is mentioned; another stinger and "Deutschland über alles" (in the trombones, minor key) intervene when the Germans are mentioned; neutral music[9] accompanies the table dispersing; "As Time Goes By" is quoted when mentioned again by Ilsa; and a series of minor ninth chords droop with Rick as he sits down, dismayed. The strong cadence that finishes the cue is motivated formally: this scene ends the first of the film's three main divisions.

The sequence is complex. In terms of spatial anchoring, it moves from the diegetic to point-of-view to non-diegetic. The diegetic music switches irregularly onscreen and off, and the sound level is realistic. The symphonic music has an appropriate dynamic level for its degree of narrative intrusion. "Avalon" is musically discontinuous and open (only a fragment is performed), "As Time Goes By" is continuous and open (most of one chorus is performed but Sam is cut off before he is finished), and Steiner's cue is discontinuous and closed (a melodramatic cue with a strong closing cadence). Editing and musical design interact only in cue 4, 7.

The music is clearly motivated throughout: Ilsa asks Sam to play; he begins "Avalon" and then she specifically asks him to play (and sing) "As Time Goes By"; cue 4, 7 is initially motivated by the stinger chord itself (by convention, music follows on this specialized sound effect). To the question of whether the music is strongly coded: "Avalon" is similar to the earlier song performances, but "As Time Goes By" is immediately turned into a cinematic code for the Paris romance of Rick and Ilsa. Among the cultural musical codes embedded in cue 4, 7 are the dissonant stinger, the minor key at the opening (and descending stepwise bass from tonic to dominant), the waltz affect (as code for Paris, elegance, or pleasurable social environment), the minor key and trombones for "Deutschland," the tritone placement of the "Time" quote against "Deutschland," the neutral affect, the final three-chord cadence, and the color shift in the final chord from minor to major (anticipating the next morning's interview in Renault's office).

The performances in sequences 1–3 are all café background music; as such they establish a neutral midpoint from which the later ones diverge. Corinna Mura's performance is strongly public, foregrounded (even though narrative advancement is not deferred during the performance), but Dooley Wilson's subsequent performances are very private; indeed, it is uncertain whether other café patrons can hear them. Mura first appears in a high angle shot (with the spotlight, as it were), but the camera cuts away from her to conversation between Laszlo and Ilsa, so that her performance becomes backgrounded in the same way (and at the same sound level) as the band's previous numbers. The temporary foregrounding, however, presages the next sequence, as Sam performs for Ilsa, framed by her requests and interruptions. His performance of "Avalon" is undermined by dialogue, but "As Time Goes By" is not; instead the camera settles on an extended close-up of Ilsa as she internalizes his performance. Cuts to long shots and the return of café noise signal her return to awareness of her surroundings as Rick approaches. When the music dives back into point-of-view after the stinger chord, the symphonic music functions as the source music did a moment earlier.

As the preceding, brief account suggests, music's characteristics and narrative functions may perhaps be described more effectively if we separate the diegetic/non-diegetic from narrational foregrounding/backgrounding. To avoid confusion caused by double usage (background music is not necessarily backgrounded), the semiotic terms "marked" and "unmarked" will be employed as these have been adapted to music by Robert Hatten (1994). Briefly, the unmarked term provides the conventional framework of the "expected" against which the marked term stands out as uncommon and therefore capable of being endowed with specific expressive meaning; for example, in eighteenth-century music, the expressive nature of the uncommon minor key is set against the backdrop of the conventional major, or chromatic progressions against the conventional diatonic.[10]

The terms are combined and depicted as a set of logical oppositions in figure 3.[11] The initial term appears at the upper left: the "marked diegetic" is a performance that is highlighted, brought out as the primary activity, such as a production number in a musical. To the right of the marked diegetic is an opposing term, "non-diegetic; marked," which refers to underscoring brought to the attention of the spectator by means of unusually loud sound levels, abrupt entrance, close synchronization with the image track (mickey-mousing), or associations of leitmotive or affect. Under this definition, much of the underscoring in classical Hollywood feature films is marked non-diegetic; as Max Steiner put it, "There is a tired old bromide in this business to the effect that a good film score is one you don't hear. What good is it if you don't notice it?" (Thomas 1991, 71–72). What this term measures is a basic feature of sound cinema: the tension between image track and sound track, and within the sound track between music and dialogue. In fact even Steiner's scores do not draw attention to themselves constantly. Perhaps a better description of the marked non-diegetic is underscoring that is foregrounded. Thus, mickey-mousing, motivic quotes, or affect cues are not automatically marked: they become so only when their level of intrusion into the narrative is high. For example, the stinger chord that begins cue 4, 7 is certainly marked non-diegetic: the sound level is high, the entrance is very abrupt (after a long absence of underscoring), the chord is both synchronized and affective (it catches the look of surprise on Rick's face and it measures the shock). The neutral music that accompanies the party breaking up lies at the opposite extreme: low dynamic level, no obvious motivic quotes, neutral affect. Where underscoring is clearly subordinate to the image track, then the former's normal condition should be the logical contrary of the initial term: not-diegetic, unmarked (as shown at the lower right of figure 3). The diagram is completed with the logical contrary of the marked non-diegetic, or the unmarked diegetic, a term which aptly describes the performances in sequences 1–3: non-highlighted set performances by the café's dance band.

The nexus of four terms just described is sufficient to begin breaking down the authority of the diegetic/non-diegetic. If music can be marked by intrinsic properties such as dynamic levels or instrumentation, then those properties may achieve a status equal to or greater than that of the diegetic/non-diegetic. In other words, music may be foregrounded or backgrounded — marked or unmarked — independently of its spatial anchoring. In the *Casablanca* examples, the diegetic/non-diegetic was undermined in three principal ways. First, both terms serve the same narrative functions. The dance-band music served as background music for the majority of the sequences, and sound levels were adjusted accordingly; the latter did not follow some "realistic" aesthetic that would have aimed to replicate the sound characteristics of a physical space. Both diegetic and non-diegetic music was used effectively for point-of-view purposes and for title associations: "Deutschland über alles" (cue 4, 7) in

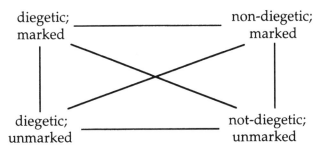

Figure 3 Semiotic square depicting logical relations based on diegetic/non-diegetic and markedness

this sense acts in exactly the same way as "Heaven Can Wait"; the menace in the former's quotation comes from its setting, not from anything intrinsic to the tune. Second, the diegetic/non-diegetic pair is undermined because it is not the only — or even the most important — aspect of music in most of these sequences. The performances here were all complex: none was simply, unequivocally, and entirely diegetic or non-diegetic. The diegetic music was not often marked, and the diegetic/non-diegetic status itself seemed to be controlled less often by simple spatial anchoring (performers onscreen) than by manipulation of sound levels. In sequences 1–3, furthermore, the song-title associations made more of a contribution to narrative than did the diegetic status of the music. Third, the indifference to musical style in the diegetic/non-diegetic pair suggests that style is not a trait closely associated with them. Granted, musical styles can certainly be constrained by narrative requirements (it is unlikely — though not impossible — that Rick's Café would have a band of strings and woodwinds) or by genre conventions (it is unlikely in films of this period that the dance band would play the melodramatic cue 4, 7, with its stinger chords and leitmotivic development). But there is nothing to prevent the dance-band music from acting as non-diegetic (a state it closely approaches at many points during sequences 1–3, as we have seen) nor the symphonic music from functioning diegetically (as it very nearly does in the "internal diegetic" or point-of-view passages).

It would seem apparent, then, that the integrated sound track is more complex than a simple alternation between the terms of the pair "realistic"/"unrealistic." Just as the directors and film editors of the twenties exploited and perfected the art of intercutting, which compromised the "realism" of a stationary camera shot (as if the camera represented the viewer standing in place), the sound designers of the later thirties were not interested in merely duplicating the sound characteristics of depicted physical spaces (Altman 1992b, 54–56); they were concerned with sound as narrational strategy. We may, therefore, challenge the notion of a diegetic film theory itself. An ancient Greek word appropriated to film theory as a synonym for "story," diegesis "has come to be the accepted term for the fictional world of the story" (Bordwell 1985, 16). This model is built on a language analogy, in that it assumes the story and its presentation (as plot) are "spoken" (enunciated) and ultimately controlled by a narrator, whether or not the latter can be identified as some specific individual. A fundamental problem with this model is its assumption of listener/spectator passivity, a notion which is endemic to Gorbman's account of film music. Her insistence on the priority of non-diegetic music and on its synchronization with the image track posits a passive spectator being acted upon by the film: non-diegetic music works in the background, "unheard," to lull the viewer into accepting the filmic illusion of reality

(Gorbman 1987, 5–6, 69). Although such theories of spectatorship were popular in the eighties, they are mostly discredited now (Bordwell 1989, 165–168, 255; Littlefield 1990, 166–167). Though Gorbman herself says at one point that "music . . . is constantly engaged in an existential and aesthetic struggle with narrative representation" (1987, 13), she downplays music's ability to contradict the image track and dialogue, and she ignores a viewer/listener's ability to construct a range of interpretations, a capability which would, of course, undercut both the notion of a passive spectator and the assumption of a wholly unified filmic discourse.

Bordwell proposes that we "consider film viewing a complicated, even skilled activity" (1985, 33). The theory he constructs is in a number of ways analogous to the music theory of Lerdahl and Jackendoff (1983). A particular advantage of Bordwell's approach is that it separates the active cognitive processes of the spectator (which are centered on constructing the story [1985, 48]) from judgments of value or other ideological assessments which are properly the task of critical interpretation. He replaces the diegetic model of film with one based on "formal systems [of narration] which both cue and constrain the viewer's construction of a story" (1985, 48). These include stylistic and genre conventions or schemata as well as narrational strategies that cover, among other things, range and depth of knowledge, degree of self-consciousness, and ideal rate of flow of story information. Thus, instead of emphasizing the move from diegetic to non-diegetic in the "As Time Goes By" cues, we might point to changes in range and depth of knowledge. In this scene, the range of knowledge is at first restricted (the viewer derives information from dialogue, facial expressions, and physical movements) and the depth of knowledge is shallow (consider the indifferent, aborted performance of "Avalon"). Knowledge is both less restricted and deeper when "As Time Goes By" becomes point-of-view music: the viewer has access to Ilsa's feelings, "hears" what she is thinking. The subsequent dialogue adds still more information (because of the larger number of characters involved), and the underscoring does also, since by convention it acts somewhat in the fashion of a voice-over narrator.

It is not possible to work out in this space the details of a merger of my field or network model described with the constructs in Bordwell's theory of narrative systems, but the discussion above should have been sufficient to suggest that it is desirable to unseat the diegetic/non-diegetic pair, because only by that means will song performances in the cinema be allowed a chance to receive their due. The schematic hierarchy that links the diegetic to popular music and non-diegetic to symphonic or classical music must be broken down. This is not to say that these pairings do not happen or even that they are uncommon, but they are plot elements or specific narrational tactics. Using them exclusively to build historical accounts and theoretical models produces a distorted view of the history of sound cinema and an inadequate basis for theoretical modeling and the close readings that depend on those models for their logic.

Compromising the symphonic/underscoring/classical/artistically-valued linkages will not be an easy task, however, for criticism seems bound to this schema, no matter how serious its weaknesses. To illustrate, I cite the passage with which Christopher Palmer concludes his evaluation of Erich Korngold:

Popular music of whatever genre has always had its place in films; of course it has, for film is entertainment and has to be popular. But unless it ever reaches . . . a complete nadir of non-quality and eccentricity, there will, equally, always be a place for music of a more serious intent. . . . That is one of the most marvellous things about film — its all-embracingness and diversity. It can feed on all things and, therefore, give something back to all people in return to establish its own traditions and criteria and continually refashion them. Only what is bad gets totally discarded; what is good may go out of fashion, . . . but the principle, . . . the core of quality — star quality — remains as a vital regenerative force. Of nothing is this more true than of music. (Palmer 1990, 66)

If we attempt to untangle the twists of logic in this muddled homily, we find first of all that the word "popular" is seemingly detached from its usual connotation, as in the pair classical music/popular music; at least this seems to be what Palmer means by the phrase "of whatever genre." Thus, "popular" might apply just as well to John Williams' Wagner-Korngold pastiches in *Star Wars* as to Jerome and Scholl's "Knock on Wood." However, in the second sentence, "popular" and lack of quality have once again been linked and opposed to "serious," which of course suggests higher quality but is also a synonym for "classical" (in the form "serious music"). In other words, the question of style, supposedly rooted out by a generous move in the first sentence, returns with a vengeance to separate the cultures. The two subsequent sentences find the author undaunted by the contradiction; they stress the inclusiveness of the cinema, its ability to appeal to all persons and all tastes, an ability that is elevated to the driving force in the historical processes of film evolution. Yet, if cinema is thereby allowed "to establish its own traditions and criteria and continually refashion them," the final two sentences show that cinematic history with respect to music is, nevertheless, constrained by forces external to itself. Palmer reifies those forces as the inevitable historical process by which critics and scholars "discover" the music that is intrinsically "good," the music of quality that will endure. In point of fact, of course, Palmer is simply appealing to the familiar tactic of canonization, by means of which an interpretative community establishes and enforces a hierarchy among artists and their works and thus also controls the writing of historical narratives. By contriving both to include and to exclude music other than the "serious" and symphonic, Palmer hopes to gain authority over all of cinema music at the same time he confines the possibility of quality to traditional European concert music.

Even apart from its internal contradictions, Palmer's argument cannot stand. First of all, it is based on the notion that a final judgment of quality is made independently of the film: a score is good if it can be played in the concert hall. Not only is this is a badly misplaced critical tool which ignores the point laboriously made above with respect to *Casablanca* — that music is one component of an integrated sound track — but it is useless as a way to establish the priority of symphonic music, for songs are far more readily — and far more frequently — detached from the film and performed independently than are symphonic cues. Second, one cannot simultaneously assign the highest critical status to symphonic film music (because it is like concert music) but then try to isolate it in its own category separate from contemporaneous concert music, in comparison to which it must inevitably be found wanting as stylistically conservative, elliptical, and lacking in sufficient development. Third, modernism, which is the aesthetic underpinning of the notion of autonomous (concert) music, has always dealt poorly with the theater and with stylistic eclecticism, and the invocation of some of its criteria — a clear line of historical evolution, a set of canonical works, the priority of autonomous music — must necessarily be unconvincing.

It would seem then that there is something fundamentally flawed about a model for film-music interpretation based on style differences and on modes of valuation derived from the concert hall. As James Buhler and I have written with respect to one specific stylistic dichotomy that has been fundamental to intellectual debates on European music in this century:

In refusing to take an unambiguous stand on [modernism's historiographic agenda] — the Stravinsky/Schoenberg debate [and] the closely related one on atonality — film music frees itself to offer a completely different account of late romantic style, one that is not bound up with atonality as its terminus. Unfortunately, this tale has so far been told only at the movies. (1994, 385)

I would argue, further, that the story is told not in the symphonic background music, but in the whole of the sound track.

References

Abbate, C. 1991. *Unsung Voices: Opera and Musical Narrative in the Nineteenth Century*. Princeton: Princeton University Press.

Altman, R. 1992a. "The Material Heterogeneity of Recorded Sound", in his *Sound Theory/Sound Practice*. New York and London: Routledge, 15–31.

Altman, R. 1992b. "Sound Space", in his *Sound Theory/Sound Practice*. New York and London: Routledge, 46–64.

Altman, R. 1992c. "Introduction: Sound/History", in his *Sound Theory/Sound Practice*. New York and London: Routledge, 113–125.

Bordwell, D. 1985. *Narration in the Fiction Film*. Madison: University of Wisconsin Press.

Bordwell, D. 1989. *Making Meaning: Inference and Rhetoric in the Interpretation of Cinema*. Cambridge: Harvard University Press.

Bordwell, D. and Thompson, K. 1990. *Film Art: An Introduction*. 3rd ed. New York: McGraw Hill.

Bordwell, D., Staiger, J. and Thompson, K. 1985. *The Classical Hollywood Cinema: Film Style and Mode of Production to 1960*. New York: Columbia University Press.

Brown, R. S. 1994. *Overtones and Undertones*. Berkeley: University of California Press.

Broyles, M. 1991. "Music and Class Structure in Antebellum Boston". *Journal of the American Musicological Society* 44/3: 450–493.

Buhler, J. and Neumeyer, D. 1994. "Review of Flinn", *Strains of Utopia*, and Kalinak, *Settling the Score*. *Journal of the American Musicological Society* 47/2: 364–385.

Flinn, C. 1992. *Strains of Utopia: Gender, Nostalgia, and Hollywood Film Music*. Princeton: Princeton University Press.

Geduld, H. 1975 *The Birth of the Talkies: From Edison to Jolson*. Bloomington: Indiana University Press.

Gorbman, C. 1987. *Unheard Melodies: Narrative Film Music*. Bloomington: Indiana University Press.

Greimas, A. J. and Rastier, F. 1968. "The Interaction of Semiotic Constraints". *Yale French Studies* 41, 86–105.

Handzo, S. 1985. "Appendix: A Narrative Glossary of Film Sound Technology", in Elisabeth Weis and John Belton, eds. *Film Sound: Theory and Practice*, 383–426. New York: Columbia University Press.

Harmetz, A. 1992. *Round Up the Usual Suspects: The Making of Casablanca*. New York: Hyperion.

Hatten, R. 1994. *Musical Meaning in Beethoven: Markedness, Correlation, and Interpretation*. Bloomington: Indiana University Press.

Kahn Atkins, I. 1983. *Source Music in Motion Pictures*. Rutherford, N.J.: Fairleigh Dickinson University Press.

Kalinak, K. 1992. *Settling the Score: Music and the Classical Hollywood Film*. Madison: University of Wisconsin Press.

Koszarski, R. 1990. *An Evening's Entertainment: The Age of the Silent Feature Picture, 1915–1928*. History of the American Cinema series, ed. Charles Harpole, Vol. 3. New York: Scribner's.

Lang, E. and West, G. [1920] 1970. *Musical Accompaniment of Moving Pictures: A Practical Manual for Pianists and Organists*. New York: Arno Press.

Lebo, H. 1992. *Casablanca: Behind the Scenes*. New York: Simon and Schuster.

Lerdahl, F. and Jackendoff, R. 1983. *A Generative Theory of Tonal Music*. Cambridge: MIT Press.

Littlefield, R. 1990. "Review of Gorbman, *Unheard Melodies*". *Indiana Theory Review* 11/1–2: 165–173.

Marks, M. 1990. "Film Music of the Silent Period, 1895–1924". Ph.D. dissertation, Harvard University.

Metz, C. [1975] 1985. "Aural Objects", in Elisabeth Weis and John Belton, eds. *Film Sound: Theory and Practice*, 154–61. New York: Columbia University Press.

Miller, F. 1992. *Casablanca: As Time Goes By*. Atlanta: Turner Publishing.

Mueller, J. 1985. *Astaire Dancing: The Musical Films*. New York: Wings Books.

Neumeyer, D. 1995. "Melodrama as a Compositional Resource in Early Hollywood Sound Cinema". *Current Musicology* 57: 61–94.

Palmer, C. 1990. *The Composer in Hollywood*. London and New York: Marion Boyars.

Prendergast, R. 1977. *Film Music: A Neglected Art*. New York: W. W. Norton.

Rapée, E. [1924] 1970. *Motion Picture Moods for Pianists and Organists: A Rapid Reference Collection of Selected Pieces*. New York: Arno Press.

Rosar, W. 1989. "Stravinsky and MGM", in Clifford McCarty, ed. *Film Music I*, 109–122. New York and London: Garland Publishing.

Rozsa, M. [1982] 1989. *Double Life*. New York: Wynwood Press.

Salmon, W. 1963. *Logic*. Englewood Cliffs, NJ: Prentice Hall.

Steiner, F. 1989. "What Were Musicians Saying about Movie Music during the First Decade of Sound? A Symposium of Selected Writings", in Clifford McCarty, ed. *Film Music I*, 81–107. New York and London: Garland Publishing.

Stothart, H. 1938. "Film Music", in Stephen Watts, ed. *Behind the Screen: How Films Are Made*, 139–144. New York: Dodge Publishing.

Thomas, T. 1991. *The Art and Craft of Movie Music*. Burbank: Riverwood Press.

Tootell, G. 1927. *How to Play the Cinema Organ: A Practical Book by a Practical Player*. London: W. Paxton.

Notes

1. For accounts of the period leading from the earliest sound feature films (1926) to the integrated sound track, see Geduld 1975, 103–268; Prendergast 1977, 19–34; Gorbman 1987, 31–52; Steiner 1989; Kalinak 1992, 66–110; and Neumeyer 1995. Kahn 1983, 28–50, focuses on source music specifically.
2. The issues involved include not only the distinction between film and concert music, but also Europe and America, New York and Los Angeles, conservatory composers versus "commercial boys" (Rozsa 1982, 111), and pre-World-War-II and post-World-War-II generations. For an example of the errors and misrepresentations that can easily result from taking too hard a position about these issues, see Palmer 1990, 19–27.

3. My information comes primarily from cue sheets for productions by United Artists and Selznick Productions, plus a few each from Republic Pictures, MGM, and Warner Bros. I do not have information about the practices of Paramount, Columbia, or other companies.

4. This information comes from business records housed in the Warner Bros. Collection, University of Southern California. The prices involved are rather high (which probably influenced Forbstein's decision not to use the song) — Warner's paid only $500 for visual vocal use of "Shine," which took the spot intended for "Old Man Mose," and $1000 for unlimited use of "As Time Goes By" (a sum which was paid to Harms, Inc., a music publishing company owned by Warners).

5. By "theater orchestra" I mean the hybrid group that is basically a dance band augmented with a relatively small number of string instruments.

6. On some of the historical sources for the harsh distinction between the classical and the popular in American musical culture, see Broyles 1991. For a chronological account of the ways in which critics and scholars of film music have tried to address its special cultural and genre problems, see Marks 1990, 12–44.

7. On the issue of synchronization versus counterpoint, see Buhler and Neumeyer 1994, 372–377.

8. Amazingly, the performance of "Knock on Wood" is similarly broken up by intercutting — but not dialogue — despite the fact that the studio hoped to exploit this newly written song as a possible hit-parade moneymaker (Miller 1992, 159).

9. The term "neutral" is a specific term derived from silent-film affect categories (Rapée [1924], iii).

10. Hatten develops this notion much further (1994, 29–66) but the descriptions given here are sufficient for the present purpose.

11. The opposing terms (across the top of Figure 2) are called "contraries" in logic; the diagonally related terms are called "contradictories" (Salmon 1963 101; Greimas and Rastier 1968, 87–88).

Contemporary Music Review
2000, Vol. 19, Part 1, pp. 63–87
Reprints available directly from the publisher
Photocopying permitted by license only

Analyzing Third Stream

David Joyner

This article offers a music-historical context in which to evaluate the success of third-stream music (c. 1945–65). The claims made in favor of this hybrid fusion of jazz and classical music styles are examined, especially those of Gunther Schuller. The article argues that third stream ultimately failed to realize the often lofty goals of its most vigorous proponents due its tendency not to "swing" and to its strong attenuation of improvisatory freedom that jazz traditionally allots to soloists.

KEYWORDS: Jazz, third stream, Gunther Schuller, Stan Kenton, birth of Cool band

Defining Third Stream

In 1987, Gunther Schuller defined third-stream music as follows:

Third stream. A term coined by Gunther Schuller, in a lecture at Brandeis University in 1957, for a type of music which, through improvisation or written composition or both, synthesizes the essential characteristics and techniques of contemporary Western art music and various ethnic or vernacular musics. At the heart of this concept is the notion that any music stands to profit from a confrontation with another; thus composers of Western art music can learn a great deal from the rhythmic vitality and swing of jazz, while jazz musicians can find new avenues of development in the large-scale forms and complex tonal systems of classical music. (Schuller 1987, 377)

Schuller celebrates, in this passage at least, the synthetic character of third stream, casting it as a powerful blend of the art-music and jazz traditions. According to Schuller, both art music and jazz have something to gain by such a stylistic "confrontation" with one another. But despite such elegant articulations of its aesthetic goals by widely respected jazz scholars like Schuller, third-stream music has remained a controversial endeavor since its inception; perhaps no other style in jazz has been the subject of such divided response among critics, players, and listeners both inside and outside of the world of jazz. For much of its history, third-stream music has seemed to be caught uncomfortably between the worlds of Western European art music and jazz, at times apparently unwelcome in either world and thus causing its practitioners and advocates to fight an aesthetic battle on two fronts simultaneously.

But the idea of blending jazz and classical music did not begin with third stream. In grappling with the question of defining third-stream music and tracing its heritage, Robert Loran Brown, Jr. has developed a helpful classification of this classical/jazz hybrid music by considering aspects of historical context, intent, and technical approach (Brown 1974). Third stream's roots can actually be found in earlier styles of American music; accordingly, Brown's first category of assimilative music is ragtime, epitomized by the compositions of Scott Joplin. The second is a practice he calls "jazzing the classics"; this category includes both jazz-styled renderings of classical repertoire as well as jazz imitation of classical styles. Brown's third category identifies jazz music that utilizes performance media usually associated with classical music, such as traditionally non-jazz instrumentation (i.e. strings, bassoon, oboe) or electronic computer or tape music. A fourth category encompasses jazz pieces that employ quasi-classical concepts such as programmatic music, extended forms or traditional classical formal models, and serial techniques. Brown rearranges and elaborates on these categories somewhat when he presents his attempt at a strictly historical order of assimilation, and arrives at the following succession of styles: 1) ragtime, 2) jazzing the classics, 3) stylistic imitations of classical music, 4) symphonic jazz, 5) West coast, cool school, and ultimately 6) third stream. Brown, however, does not provide specific dates for each of the periods he enumerates, and a closer look at Brown's parsing reveals a considerable chronological overlap between categories. Categories 1, 2, and 4 were essentially products of the time period from about 1897 to 1930. Category 3 covers virtually the entire history of jazz. Categories 5 and 6 involve a time period from about the mid-1940s to the end of the 1960s.

Brown's categorization — despite the absence of a tidy historical succession — remains a useful point of departure for an overview of what Joseph Stuessy (1977) has termed "confluent music" — the incorporation of jazz and classical music by either stylistic camp in any era. The main focus of this article will be a consideration of the many issues and problems associated with confluence in jazz generally, and in third-stream music specifically; a significant amount of discussion will be devoted to third stream below. But in order to provide a music-stylistic and -historical context in which third stream may be situated, we will first briefly review the history and general characteristics of those styles that lead to third stream according to Brown's interpretation. I will generally employ the term "classical" music for the sake of brevity in terminology in referring to what is known variously as "European art music," "notated art music," or any combination or derivation thereof as practiced mostly by composers in Europe and the United States.

Ragtime

Ragtime was the first significant infiltration of an authentic African-American music into the mainstream of popular music, and it flourished from approximately 1895 until the mid-1920s. Ragtime was also the first form-conscious African-American music. It was modeled after the march, with three or four sixteen-bar themes, each repeated once, the third usu· ally modulating up the interval of a fourth. It was a sturdy design that remained prominent in the jazz repertoire until the 1930s. Ragtime's greatest composer — and certainly the composer most often associated with the style — was Scott Joplin (1867–1917), who codified the form and style of "classic ragtime" with his "Maple Leaf Rag" in 1899. Joplin also aspired to rise above the realm of popular entertainment and establish himself as the first black "classicist." To this end, he composed two operas and a ballet and, all the while, increasingly complex piano rags that were for the most part too musically sophisticated for the popular audience. The most remarkable of these later rags is Joplin's "Euphonic Sounds" (1909), particularly its startling second strain.

The tonal focus of this rag moves almost immediately from B♭ major to B minor. In the fifth measure, the harmony moves quickly from a V^7 of E♭ major to vii° of C minor. By the ninth bar the tonal center is G minor, D♭ major by the thirteenth bar, and back to V^7 of B♭ major by the fifteenth bar. Coupled with these rapid-fire shifts of key center are complementary dynamic contrasts that provide a sense of a complex multi-thematic work, all in the course of a mere sixteen measures. Here one clearly sees that Joplin was pushing at the music-technical boundaries of popular music, and the result is a rag that was probably difficult for many pop listeners to appreciate.

Joplin's most ambitious work was his opera *Treemonisha* (1911), a combination of ragtime, operetta, parlor songs, and black folk music. Typical of the situation that later befell much third-stream and other confluent efforts, *Treemonisha* could not find an audience. Rudi Blesh and Harriet Janis, in their pioneering history *They All Played Ragtime*, report on the one meager performance in Harlem: "The musical drama made virtually no impression... its special quality in any event would surely have been lost on the typical Harlem audience that attended. The listeners were sophisticated enough to reject their folk past, but not sufficiently to relish a return to it in art" (Blesh and Janis 1950).

Jazzing the Classics

A typical practice throughout the history of ragtime and jazz has been lending a syncopated or jazz treatment to classical works, sometimes motivated more by novelty than earnest musical exploration. New Orleans pianists Tony Jackson and Ferdinand "Jelly Roll" Morton would often render ragtime versions of operatic selections in the Storyville brothels, excerpts such as the "Miserere" from Verdi's *Il Trovatore*. Vaudeville ragtime artist Ben Harney performed ragtime versions of Mendelssohn's "Spring Song." Harlem stride pianist James P. Johnson ragged Rachmaninoff's "Prelude in C# Minor," while pianist Eubie Blake syncopated Wagner's overture to *Tannhäuser*. These examples date back to the earliest days of ragtime and jazz (1897–1925).

This practice of jazzing the classics has continued over the years, though these later efforts were mostly not intended as humorous novelty numbers and were often more serious in their motivation. French jazz artists in the 1950s and 60s seemed particularly fascinated with the idea of performing European art music in a jazz style. Consider, for instance, the work of the Jacques Loussier Trio, with Loussier playing straight renditions of Bach on the piano underpinned by jazz bass and drums. The (Ward) Swingle Singers and their predecessor, The Double Six of Paris, also recorded performances of Bach works with a swing beat. In the United States, there was Bill Evans and Claus Ogerman's 1965 recording for Verve Records (*Bill Evans Trio with Symphony Orchestra* Verve V68640), which featured easy-listening jazz renditions of works by Bach, Chopin, Scriabin, and Fauré. British pianist and percussionist Victor Feldman recorded jazz renditions of Chopin in the 1970s and pianist Bob James did jazz versions of Rameau in the 1980s.

Stylistic Imitations of Classical Music

Another area of jazz/classical confluence is the stylistic imitation of classical music. This can involve several aspects, some more superficial than others. Often one finds the employment of what would popularly be considered non-jazz, or marginally jazz instruments, i.e. strings (other than double bass), double-reed instruments, french horn, or timpani. This will often suffice for some listeners or critics to consider a group or performance as a jazz/classical hybrid. Paul Whiteman's orchestra, prominent in the 1920s and 30s, was comprised of orchestral instruments (strings, double reeds, harp) in addition to jazz instruments such as the saxophone and banjo. Later recordings — among the many that might be cited — are Pete Rugolo's *Reeds in Hi-Fi* (Mercury MG 20260), or the Jack Marshall Sextet's album *18th-Century Jazz* (Columbia), on which the group uses early-music instrumentation to play jazz standards. Both of these recordings are from the 1950s; in the mid to late 1950s one can look to the jazz brass-choir recordings of Gunther Schuller and J. J. Johnson, as well as to the Gil Evans/Miles Davis wind-orchestra recordings, all of these for Columbia records.

A second area of classical stylistic imitation would be long, programmatic jazz works that may give the impression of an integrated epic piece, but are most often a series of short works with extended improvisations and linked by a prevailing extra-musical theme. Beginning in the 1930s but more prevalent in the 1950s and early 1960s, this approach would include many of the suites and other extended works by Duke Ellington (*The Far East Suite* (1966), *The Queen's Suite* (1962), *Such Sweet Thunder* (1957) and Charles Mingus (*The Black Saint and the Sinner Lady* (1963), *Epitaph* (1962)).

The musical conceptions of Duke Ellington (1899–1974) were highly personal vehicles that both expressed his own imagination and begged for musical comment from his bandmembers. The success of Ellington was not his ability to mimic the classical tradition; he was no more interested in that than he was in upholding a jazz tradition. His success was in extending the range of his musical vocabulary by coalescing the totality of his musical environment and manifesting it in an unpretentious, unselfconscious way that swung to the satisfaction of the jazz community and yet captured the imagination of the classical community.

From the 1930s on, Ellington wrote a number a long works in a variety of forms. Most are suites, a collection of four or five minutes pieces linked programmatically, but Ellington also wrote lengthy multi-section single pieces. The earliest and most celebrated is his 1935 work *Reminiscing in Tempo*, an elegy for his mother. This thirteen-minute piece, filling four 78-r.p.m. record sides, stands out from other longer Ellington works in that it shows perhaps the finest formal and developmental control he ever exercised. He avoids the multi-thematic and multi-(short) movement, and the extension through improvisation paradigm of myriad extended jazz works, including many of his own. "Reminiscing" is restricted to one main theme, a secondary theme, a couple of transitional passages, and a four-chord vamp. The main theme appears fourteen times in the course of the piece, with only three of the iterations exhibiting any variation in melodic character. Ellington casts the theme in a variety of keys, registers, harmonic contexts, and instrumentation. He drew heavily upon his intimate knowledge of the unique tonal quality of his individual band members for his developmental decisions. He did not, however, draw upon their improvisational input, using only pre-scribed solos (Schuller 1989, 76–8). Ellington continued his assault on the regularity of the four-bar phrase in "Reminiscing," creating twenty and thirty-bar structures subdivided into groups of ten, fourteen, and eighteen measures. These phrasing irregularities add to the overall effect of seam-lessness, and they participate in Ellington's balancing of predictable and unpredictable elements as the piece unfolds. Another notable work in this form is *The Tattooed Bride* from 1948, which consistently employs a brief motive throughout the entire thirteen-minute work.

Charles Mingus was the next major jazz composer to routinely use extended form in jazz. Gunther Schuller, in fact, credits Mingus with coining the term "extended form." In Mingus's case, form was usually extended by the improvisations of his band members. Mingus was very much influenced by the compositions of Duke Ellington, but more by Ellington's idiosyncratic use of harmony, orchestration, and creative interaction with his sidemen than with his propensity for jazz composi-tions beyond the perfunctory four-minute limit. Unlike Ellington, Mingus did have the opportunity to study classical composition in his youth and, as early as 1939, wrote *The Chill of Death*, a brooding piece for narrator and orchestra that he did not have recorded until 1971, when it was included on the Columbia album, *Let My Children Hear Music* (CK 48910). After 1955, Mingus resolved to abandon the practice of extensively notat-ing his compositions, electing to teach them to his performers by rote. A notable exception in this regard was *Revelations*, commissioned by Gunther Schuller for inclusion in the 1957 Brandeis Summer Festival.

Mingus, like Ellington, did not seek to imitate classical models, but to bend the rules of jazz form in his day. He used the AABA form of the American popular song, but with asymmetrical phrase groupings such as 8, 16, 14, 8. He also sought to use more polyphonic and heterophonic counterpoint than is usually found in the more common homophonic tex-ture of jazz. In rarer cases, jazz composers have employed traditional forms drawn from classical music such as fugue or developmental tech-niques from dodecaphonic composition, and these can be found particu-larly in the work of John Lewis, John Carisi, and Gunther Schuller.

Symphonic Jazz

The confluent approach that is best known, and the most infamous in both jazz and classical circles, is the so-called "symphonic jazz" approach of the 1920s. The chief proponent was bandleader Paul Whiteman, who engineered a successful blend of society dance music, jazz, and classical music. He had a massive dance orchestra of around thirty-five instrumentalists, including harp, strings, and woodwinds. Whiteman's music was an effort intended to "make a lady out of jazz" by diluting the features of jazz rhythm and improvisation and legitimizing jazz with occasional interpolations of Wagner, Stravinsky, or Debussy. This popular combination culminated with the commission and premiere of George Gershwin's "Rhapsody in Blue" at Aeolian Hall in 1924, the climax of a program Whiteman called "An Experiment in Modern Music." The idea of legitimizing jazz by Europeanizing it also influenced some of New York's black jazz composers. To cite a single exemplary event, there was a 1928 concert at Carnegie Hall that featured the premiere of Harlem stride pianist James P. Johnson's "Yamekraw," an extended piece for piano and orchestra similar in form and concept to Gershwin's "Rhapsody."

The symphonic jazz efforts of the 1920s are indicative of the mindset of many jazz musicians of the day. Among these musicians there was a yearning to command the large forms found in classical music. At the time, improvisation was a relatively new concept and thus one that very few musicians had mastered. Many musicians and audiences were intolerant to the idea of improvisation, holding to the notion that notated music was controlled — and thereby better — music. There was a prevailing feeling that jazz was a comparatively inferior music that had to graft on elements of European art music to lend it legitimacy; it should aspire to take on the refined image of classical music in some way, even if it was only in the style of its staging in performance.

West Coast Cool Jazz

The "West Coast," "cool," and third-stream jazz movements began in the 1940s and continued to about the mid-1960s. The mid-1940s saw the redefinition of jazz as high art rather than popular music, and this occurred with the emergence of "bebop." Jazz soon saw an influx of predominately white jazz composers, arrangers, and instrumentalists, some of whom were trained in contemporary classical-music techniques. While others were self-taught or mentored outside the academy, both groups shared modernist aesthetic tendencies and sought new approaches to jazz. One group of these new modernist writers came from the Claude Thornhill band, a moderately successful big band that began integrating streamlined bebop lines and Ellingtonian orchestration into its canon. Thornhill's arrangers included Gerry Mulligan, John Carisi, and their patriarch Gil Evans. These arrangers teamed with Miles Davis in 1949 to form a nonet, a smaller version of the Thornhill band, known in later years as the "Birth of the Cool" band.

The Birth of Cool band was a pivotal event in the development of third-stream music. In the first place, it brought together prominent musicians from several different jazz endeavors. The group's leader, Miles Davis, had begun his career with Charlie Parker four years earlier and, at twenty-four, was already an elder statesman in bebop. Konitz, Mulligan, Gil Evans, french hornist Sandy Siegelstein, and tubist Bill Barber were Thornhill veterans. John Lewis and Kenny Clarke were recently of the Dizzy Gillespie big band and Lewis would subsequently form the Modern Jazz Quartet, the band Schuller felt personified the third-stream ideal. The Birth of Cool group recorded for Capitol Records, a relatively new Los Angeles label tied closely to Stan Kenton, and the label that recorded Lennie Tristano's historic small group recordings at about the same time. The band was essentially a writer's workshop, emphasizing the written arrangement at a time when the enthusiasm for unencumbered improvisation was at a fever pitch. The group got a tepid reception at the time, recording only a dozen sides and playing a mere three weeks at a half empty Royal Roost in New York. But the seed for third stream was planted in New York, particularly in the mind of French hornist Gunther Schuller, who played his first jazz gig with the Birth of Cool band.

Modernist musical behavior and confluent activity was also to be found on the West Coast; its chief proponent was the Stan Kenton orchestra of Los Angeles, the most unique and longest lasting emblem of classical/jazz confluence and probably the first example of the third-stream concept proper. At a time when most big bands were dead or dying, Kenton created a forty-piece orchestra devoted entirely to explorative compositions by a team of visionary writers. This particular group, the "Innovations" orchestra (which folded in 1951), ended up personally costing Kenton $200,000; nonetheless, Kenton continued undaunted with several incarnations of his band until his death in 1979. No one, with the exception of Duke Ellington, showed such longevity and steadfast high-mindedness as did Stan Kenton.

Like Duke Ellington, Stan Kenton (1911–1979) knew how to balance making commercial hits with artistic pursuits, using the former to subsidize the latter. What set him apart was his ability to sell his artistic wares to the general public. Even at his most uncompromising, he filled concert halls with people, making it fashionable to be a discriminating listener to esoteric music. For all the musical and financial chances he took, he still died a millionaire. The popular successes of Boyd Raeburn, Claude Thornhill, and Dizzy Gillespie, big band leaders and contemporaries of Kenton following the same musical path, were much more short-lived by comparison. Kenton's prime motivation was his vision of what a concert jazz orchestra should be: a big, loud jazz orchestra.

Kenton dubbed his music "progressive jazz," a tongue-in-cheek working title that stuck because no one could come up with anything better. Pete Rugolo recalled, "It caused a whole new thing in music. It was the first time anyone wrote music that sounded very modern, like Stravinsky and Bartók...Bernstein...[and] Milhaud, whom I studied with. Nobody had that kind of sound before in jazz or big band music. I wrote 5/4 bars, 3/4 bars, 1/4 bars" (Daryll 1992).

It is only coincidental that Kenton's propensity for modernism was realized when bebop was just coming to full flower in New York. Kenton was based in Los Angeles and his modernist investigations developed far from the New York influence of Dizzy Gillespie, Duke Ellington, John Lewis, or any of the other East Coast "modernists." His stylistic lineage actually stemmed from the intricate writing found in the Jimmie Lunceford band. Lunceford, in turn, had studied "out west" in Denver with Wilberforce Whiteman, father of "symphonic jazz" king Paul Whiteman. (Lunceford's startling 1934 composition "Stratosphere" exemplifies the character of this western United States stylistic family tree.) And, though it is a popular belief that migrating New York cool-schoolers brought their style with them to the West, several of Kenton's sidemen, such as Lennie Niehaus and Shorty Rogers, were already establishing a concomitant style when the Easterners arrived.

The writers Kenton used were as far removed from the New York modernist scene as he was. Pete Rugolo studied with Darius Milhaud at Mills College in Oakland, California (as did Dave Brubeck and Cal Tjader). Bill Russo was a Chicagoan who studied with Lennie Tristano. Bill Holman studied at the Westlake College of Music in Los Angeles. Robert Graettinger, another Westlake student who studied extensively with studio arranger Russell Garcia, was the most enigmatic of Kenton's composers. He epitomized the intensity of Kenton's commitment to modernism — with or without deference to jazz style — in his 1948 (rev. 1951) composition *City of Glass*.

In fact, the most dangerous aspect of Kenton to the jazz mainstream of the 1940s was that he rendered eastern bebop almost irrelevant. It is not that Kenton was naive about bop or that he rejected it. His constituents also included Lee Konitz, Gerry Mulligan, Stan Getz, and Gil Evans, some of the most important figures of the New York "cool school." There was tenor saxophonist Vido Musso, veteran of the Benny Goodman band. He also had some of the most formidable bop stylists from the West Coast, particularly alto saxophonists Charlie Mariano and Art Pepper, trombonist Frank Rosolino, and drummer Shelly Manne. Bebop, however, was an addendum to a notion Kenton had been holding since the 1930s:

It is a fact that in the minds of many of us in creative music that the modern symphonic composer and the composer whose heritage is jazz use many of the same techniques in the process of composition. The difference in the end result lies in the interpretation of the work. The same music performed by a symphonic orchestra will have and entirely different dimension when played by jazz musicians. (Kenton 1951)

The confluent styles surveyed thus far exhibit a couple of common characteristics. From the late 1890s until the mid-1940s, there was a prevailing feeling in ragtime and jazz that association with the classical music tradition was the means by which to legitimize African-American music. Musicians in these early years were consciously seeking to attach a "classical" persona to their ragtime and jazz music. While it is nice to think that such efforts were made in order to create better and more interesting music, it is more likely that the confluence was motivated by novelty or by an apologetic self-consciousness or defensiveness intent on raising the fledgling jazz music to the long-standing stature of the European art music tradition. Overall, early confluent efforts sought to win over a certain audience, one of considerably higher social position and influence than the proletariat with which jazz had already connected.

After the dawn of bebop-style jazz in the mid-1940s, the context and motivation of confluent music had evolved. Jazz, in the form of bebop, had established itself as a notable art music apart from the European tradition. Here the exploration of classical/jazz hybrids was driven more by the sincere curiosity and creativity of the musicians rather than by the need to reach the popular audience or to establish an "artsy" image. Additionally, the European art-music approaches utilized in confluent jazz from the 1940s on, such as twelve-tone or atonal techniques, appealed to a much smaller audience than the more popular late Romantic and French Impressionist styles that were prevalent in earlier confluent jazz. If audience appeal was the motivation in later confluent jazz, then it was understood that the audience was reduced, for the most part, to other musicians. In fact, confluent music from this point period forward exhibits a pressing need to be viewed as musically erudite, to shed the role or image of jazz as popular music. At the same time, confluent composers wanted to make it clear that the combining of European art music and jazz was a union of two musics of equal artistic weight, that one style would not *improve* the other, but that any musical style would, as Schuller states in his definition of third stream, "stand to profit from a confrontation with another."

Third Stream

Having presented a brief historical and stylistic overview of confluence in jazz, the remainder of this study will focus on third-stream music. I suggest, along with Brown, that third-stream music is best viewed as a confluent effort of a particular era, one that raised aesthetic and artistic questions for its time and reflected the particular motivations of its creators. Chronologically, I will view the period from the mid-1940s to the mid-1960s as the prime years for third-stream practice as Schuller originally saw it, noting the emergence of third stream from the context of bebop and West Coast jazz activities. I take the mid-1960s as the end of the third-stream era proper because, by that time, rock had so marginalized jazz *and* classical music that the issues and importance of the classical/jazz confluent effort came to be minimalized and so too, the musical activity that went with it. It is not coincidental that rock, having come of age at this time and assuming jazz's role as classical music's perceived popular music nemesis and artistic "wanna-be," took up the investigation of hybridizing with classical music itself. This conspicuously began with the Beatles' watershed *Sgt. Pepper's Lonely Hearts Club Band* in 1967 and continued primarily in Britain with the "progressive-rock" efforts of Yes, King Crimson, Emerson Lake & Palmer, and others.

I will limit my discussion to those generally considered to be "jazz" musicians, with the exception of Gunther Schuller, whom I do not consider a jazz musician but rather a knowledgeable and active participant, spokesman, and aesthetic advocate of the movement.

History, Aesthetics and Cultural Issues of Third Stream

Third-stream music really did not work; no one would let it. The idea of combining elements of notated European art music with jazz style and improvisation seemed perfectly logical to its practitioners; for, by 1957, many jazz musicians saw "classical" music and jazz as kindred musics within the realm of high art. Both musical cultures were responding to a general post-war modernism movement in the arts, striving for both complexity and social elitism (Bürger 1984). What better offspring could result than one born from such a union?

Unfortunately, many critics, musicians, and listeners viewed this creation as a mutt — a dangerous half-breed that threatened the pedigree of each musical tradition. Interestingly, the majority of this rancor came not from conservative advocates of art-music culture, but rather from voices within the jazz community. Rather than bringing about the kind of cultural synthesis its advocates intended, third-stream music exacerbated bitterness over the long-standing struggle of blacks to validate their art within the mainstream of American culture against the prevailing esteem of European art music in the public consciousness. The idea of infusing jazz with classical music elements seemed to once again insinuate that the former needed the latter for that validation, that the European musical tradition was still the standard by which all music should be judged. Yet, it is undeniable that black jazz modernists " . . . borrowed liberally from concert styles and practices. By the 1960s, free musicians had transformed the modernist aesthetic for their own uses, recasting it to assert a specifically black-oriented artistry" (Radano 1993, 109).

In truth, Schuller and other proponents of third-stream music had a genuine need to create and perform *art* music. To state it again, they saw jazz and classical music similarly as art (as opposed to popular music), so they combined them, hoping for a music that was thoughtful, well-crafted, and original. For these jazz musicians and composers, third stream would be the sum total of their experience in both stylistic realms, and thus — they hoped — would be judged on its own merits and not by its ability to uphold any one tradition.

Far overriding the notion of correcting a fault in one idiom with a virtue from another was the need for jazz musicians to disassociate their music from crass commercialism, its function merely as dance music and, above all, to rescue both musical traditions from stasis by dismantling public stereotypes and expectations, leaving the way open for uninhibited musical exploration. As Stan Kenton told jazz writer Nat Hentoff:

Jazz for a long time was mixed up with pop music. Now, as it has always been in Europe, jazz is being differentiated from pop music as well as classical music. The modernists deserve the credit for proving that jazz doesn't have to be danced to . . . As a matter of fact, I don't think jazz was meant to continue as dance music. People got the idea just because it was confused with pop music . . . Jazz has to develop; it can't always remain functional dance music. (Hentoff 1952, 6)

This distinction from popular music was, of course, not nearly as urgent in twentieth-century art music; modernist classical music certainly struggled for public understanding and acceptance, but its identity as art — even when it was called bad art — has infrequently been in question. The struggle of jazz to define its position along a continuum that might be drawn between popular music and art, however, reaches back to its earliest years. Emerging into public consciousness as a novelty dance music in 1917 and for years thereafter using popular songs and night clubs for performance vehicles and venues, jazz was typecast as popular music, and was consequently accused of "getting above its raising" (to quote a Ricky Skaggs song) when it opted for artistic pursuit. Schuller, however, sees in this a tendency of Americans to underestimate their own musics:

[We Americans] have suffered for a long time (and still do to some extent) from a tremendous inferiority complex about our own music. That's partially understandable when one realizes that we are a very young country and we had, in fact, to import our musical traditions primarily from Europe in order to have any . . . But I think those days are long gone now, and I think it's high time that America be quite proud of its musical traditions.... (Hasse 1985, 198–199)

American classical music has, in fact, also been subject to such underestimation, and it too struggled for aesthetic legitimacy earlier in the century. Young composers such as Aaron Copland, Roger Sessions, Roy Harris, and Walter Piston fought against the critical and public indifference to European-style art music by American composers in the 1920s by forming the League of Composers. In his lively and sarcastic autobiography *A Smattering of Ignorance*, pianist Oscar Levant writes: "It is well to recall that in the early twenties, when modern music was attracting more attention in America than it ever did before, or has since, the public interest was wholly confined to European products — American music was in complete disrepute" (Levant 1940, 64). Levant goes on to say that the League "sought to establish in the East Sixties [of New York] an equivalent of the Parisian salons." One readily detects the similarity to the situation Levant describes in the bohemian bebop enclave of 52nd Street in the 1940s. Such a parallel suggests that this struggle for acceptance as serious artists was perhaps "an American thing," transcending stylistic affiliation and eventually establishing the basis for a brotherhood among some jazz and classical musicians who found themselves victims of similar cultural attitudes.

The classical music establishment voiced most of its dissension over the comingling of jazz and art music in the early part of the twentieth century — a time when America still looked to Europe for its musical values. Classical music was nurtured by wealthy American families such as the Carnegies and the Vanderbilts, as well as by music critics, journalists, and music educators. The threat of African-American music was not so much whatever competition for the attention of the public it might offer, but the more serious threat that jazz might influence and even graft on to classical music. As most historical accounts of the period run, the late nineteenth and early twentieth centuries saw the rise of intense nationalism within European music, typified by the music of composers such as Norway's Edvard Grieg, Finland's Jean Sibelius, Czechoslovakia's Antonín Dvořák, and Russia's Modest Mussorgsky and Igor Stravinsky. Advocates of nationalism within the European classical community urged the American composers to draw likewise upon their own indigenous musics and traditions; the musics of African- and Native-Americans might be employed to help establish a distinctly American nationalistic style. Some European composers even employed what they took to be American musics themselves, resulting in pieces such as Dvořák's "Symphony from the New World," Debussy's "Golliwog's Cakewalk," Stravinsky's "Ragtime for Eleven Instruments," and Darius Milhaud's "La Creation du

Monde." (Milhaud would eventually teach composition to some third-stream jazz composers at Mills College in California.) But the American art-music culture steadfastly refused to recognize its cultural distinctiveness in the blending of European and African influences, and consequently, few American composers pursued such a synthesis in earnest. Those who did, such as Aaron Copland and Samuel Barber, misguidedly drew more inspiration from syncopated vaudeville bands than from authentic jazz bands.

Ironically, this same attitude about the inherently superior quality of European music led black Americans to believe that classical music was the only worthwhile pursuit for young musicians; unfortunately, it was also clear there would be no welcome place for black musicians in the orchestra, on the opera stage, or in the recital hall at the end of such training. Barred from the culture of white art music in America, though at the same time constantly browbeaten with the perceived superiority of this music, black Americans set about establishing their own art. By the end of World War II, jazz had developed an intricate and unique harmonic practice, as well as a rhythmic system with subtleties that standard notation could not possibly capture. But perhaps most importantly, jazz took the practice of improvisation to unprecedented heights. The new jazz was dubbed "bebop" by the press; its authors were trumpeter John "Dizzy" Gillespie, saxophonist Charlie Parker, and pianist Thelonious Monk.

With the emergence of bebop, jazz fans and the classical music community now had to reassess their perceptions of jazz; its image as popular music now seemed inappropriate. The bebop jazz musicians were no longer entertaining buffoons or providers of dance music; now they were serious, artistic performers. Their music was specialized as well as technically and intellectually demanding. Some welcomed these changes in jazz, relishing the new complexity and expression. Other critics and fans were bewildered by this new jazz and abandoned bebop either for rhythm and blues, or for the establishment of a primitivist revival of early New Orleans music. But, like it or not, jazz now had a claim for recognition as art in traditional art-music aesthetic terms: it was complex absolute music that existed for its own intrinsic value, to be contemplated aesthetically in those terms alone.

Bebop was born within a tight circle of New York black artists, a community that was galvanized by the racism of the time. This socio-political *milieu* was the proud parent of a music that was capturing the imagination and respect of the world. But, as jazz historian John Litweiler observed,

The bop milieu had internalized one of the nasty features of the social tidepool in which it had spawned: intolerance. Bop musicians and audiences tended to ignore the discoveries of such eastern players as Herbie Nichols, Elmo Hope, and even, for many years, Thelonious Monk; these artists were simply peripheral to the dogmas of taste derived primarily from Charlie Parker and his successor as a model of taste, Miles Davis. (Litweiler 1992, 64)

For a moment, bebop was the radical "new thing" in jazz, delivering it from the world of popular music where, in the eyes of many, it had unfairly languished for years. But, ironically, bebop soon became the new jazz establishment, and shortly thereafter the ultra-orthodox moldy fig. Never had there been a more standardized time in jazz than during the reign of bebop. Guitarists, trombonists, and pianists — every instrumentalist, it seemed — strove to sound like Dizzy Gillespie and Charlie Parker.

Oddly enough, the most stylistically tolerant artist from the bebop camp was probably Parker himself. Though he had little formal training, he delighted in various contexts and styles of music, as exemplified in his controversial "Charlie Parker with Strings" session for Verve (MGC 501) in 1949. Many jazz afficionados and critics accused Parker of going commercial, but Parker considered it one of the high points of his career. He admired the compositions of Edgard Varèse and hoped someday to study with him. In the August 1948 issue of *Metronome* magazine, Parker commented on Stan Kenton, an already established experimenter of jazz/classical hybrids. "Kenton is the closest thing to classical music in the jazz field, if you want to call it jazz. I mean, as far as I'm concerned, there's just forms of music; people have different conceptions and different ways of presenting things. Personally, I just like to call it music, and music is what I like" (Friedwald, 1991).

Stan Kenton's music evokes extremes of opinion, either worshipful devotion or scathing criticism and hatred. Everyone will agree that subtlety is lost on the Kenton style. Both he and his orchestra were large, imposing figures. His ten man brass section (before you include the occasional section of french horns or mellophoniums) delved into the extremes of range and volume. The music was often pretentious, pompous, and overdone. Kenton believed in the adage that it was better to be hated than unnoticed. There was also the perennial accusation that his band did not swing. But, as Kenton arranger Pete Rugolo stated, "...it wasn't supposed to swing. Stan was trying to do a different kind of music... It did have a beat here and there, but it didn't always have to go 4/4. And a lot of it didn't have any beat at all. They were concert pieces with a jazz sound" (Friedwald 1991, 7).

Charlie Parker's acknowledgment of Kenton's music indicates that Parker seemed confident enough in the artistic establishment of his musical innovation, bebop, to view Kenton or classical music without malice or jealousy. Bebop and third stream music were not the same thing, but third stream did develop from the same modernist spirit that prevailed in bebop at the time. Parker apparently welcomed any serious musical investigation, including confluent music, though circumstances dictated that Parker would have little opportunity to pursue confluent projects himself. Another New York musician who would pursue confluent music, equally inspired by the work of Stan Kenton, was Gunther Schuller.

Schuller was born in 1925, son of a New York Philharmonic violinist. He was a child prodigy, developing into a formidable french horn player while still a teenager. By the age of sixteen, he was a member of the Cincinnati Symphony Orchestra, where he was the soloist for his own horn concerto. Soon afterward, he was principal horn with the Metropolitan Opera Orchestra in New York. From his earliest days, however, he had an interest in jazz. He was fascinated by the music and performances of the Duke Ellington orchestra on records and on the radio, and much of his activity outside the opera orchestra involved cruising New York's 52nd Street, epicenter of the jazz scene. Observation turned to participation in late 1949 and early 1950 when Schuller became involved in the Birth of the Cool band led by Miles Davis.

During this time Schuller divided his attention between his two musical worlds: composition in the manner of Schoenberg and Webern, and involvement with the jazz world. Schuller's involvement with jazz world was somewhat limited, however. He was never a jazz stylist, nor was he involved in jazz as a full-time occupation; he understood it, transcribed it, conducted it, wrote about it, critiqued it, and documented it, but he was never an improvisor or practitioner of the idiom in any real sense. Schuller's playing of jazz was limited to the notated score, the ensemble portions of the jazz performance. In the realm of composition, Schuller composed a series of serial classical works that incorporated jazz stylistic flavorings, the most famous being his *Seven Studies on Themes of Paul Klee* (1959), particularly the movement "Little Blue Devil."

By the mid-1950s, Schuller was actively investigating the fusion of jazz and European art-music elements. Unlike earlier jazz and classical artists, Schuller was not trying to legitimize or improve jazz, but was seeking ways to expand its possibilities, the same motivation shown by Parker, Monk, and members of the late 1940s "cool school" strain of bebop such as Lennie Tristano, Lee Konitz, Dave Brubeck and John Lewis. Schuller felt that he was synthesizing his two musical worlds.

Gunther Schuller's direction of this new confluent effort led to the occasion of the 1957 Brandeis University Festival of Creative Arts in Waltham, Massachusetts. In that year, Schuller was able to commission six confluent works from colleagues in both the jazz and classical communities. Composers from the jazz world included George Russell and Charles Mingus; those composers from the world of contemporary art music included Milton Babbitt and Harold Shapiro, and, of course, Schuller himself. In a lecture at the festival (an excerpt of which is quoted at the beginning of the present article), Schuller described the efforts of himself and his fellow composers as a "third stream" fed by the European art music and jazz streams. Intending it only as a descriptive term, the phrase "third stream" became an appellation as well as a liability for Schuller's approach to jazz.

Schuller's fellow proponent integrating European art music elements into jazz was pianist John Lewis (b. 1920). Lewis had earned a degree in music from the University of New Mexico. He met bebop drummer Kenny Clarke while in the service during World War II, who invited him to join the New York jazz scene. He became the pianist for Dizzy Gilliespie's big band and formed The Modern Jazz Quartet from its rhythm section. He was pianist for the Miles Davis "Birth of the Cool" sessions in 1949 and 1950, for which he arranged Denzil Best's "Move" and his own "Rouge." He formed an alliance with Gunther Schuller in 1948 and, together, they inaugurated a series of jazz writer's workshops in Lenox, Massachusetts. They produced a series of recordings and live performances exploring this jazz/classical fusion. In the mid-fifties, they discovered free jazz alto saxophonist and composer Ornette Coleman, whom they saw as "the new Bird" ("Bird" was Charlie Parker's nickname) and purveyor of a new practice of improvisation that would complement their compositional explorations.

Lewis attempted to provide a framework, a guide, for the soloist, a pre-scriptive pacing of stylistic and emotional contrast that the improvising soloist had little choice but to follow. He told journalist Nat Hentoff,

the audience for our work can be widened if we strengthen our work with structure . . . I do not think, however, that the sections in this structured jazz — both the improvised and writ-ten sections — should take on too much complexity. The total effect must be within the mind's ability to appreciate through the ear. Also, the music will have to swing. (Goldberg 1965, 124)

This statement reinforces the third-stream ideal: creating music of formal integrity, hopefully without impeding the spontaneity of the improvising soloist. Gunther Schuller credits Lewis and the Modern Jazz Quartet with defining the cool movement of jazz in the 1950s and implied that the compositional prowess of Lewis and the improvisational spon-taneity of vibraphonist Milt Jackson personified the third-stream ideal. Yet, while attempting to give equal credit to both form and improvisa-tion, there is an obvious self-consciousness, an apologist attitude on the part of Lewis and Schuller in the assertion that longer forms had not been employed in jazz. It is not beyond suspicion that Lewis's motivation in using traditional formal models was as much to demonstrate his know-ledge of these forms to the classical world as to seek a better type of jazz.

He seemed oblivious, however, to the "shotgun marriage" nature of the group. From Lewis' point of view, he was attempting to provide a framework for the improvising soloist. To Jackson, whose improvisational approach was right off of 52nd Street, and to much of the jazz audience, Lewis' formal roadmaps were an intrusion into the process of spontaneous improvisation. Audiences grew so tense from this aesthetic friction that in concerts they would heckle "Let Milt blow!"

In light of these events, the no-win predicament of third-stream music begins to emerge. In attempting to bring about a peaceful coexistence between musical traditions, third-stream composers brought to the forefront aesthetic clashes between the worlds of written and improvised composition in which resolution could only be hoped for in theory but never completely achieved in practice. The problem, if not the solution, is made clearer by looking at each camp's general perception of the other's shortcomings.

The ongoing "problem" with jazz, as far as the classical world was concerned, was its limitation to short, cyclic forms, such as the twelve-bar blues form or the AABA thirty-two-bar popular song form, designed by the composers and lyricists of New York's Tin Pan Alley. Another constant in jazz had been the regularity of the prescribed music's phrasing in even two-, four-, and eight-bar groupings. Bop pioneers such as Charlie Parker and Lennie Tristano consciously sought to compose and improvise irregular melodic phrases over these regular forms, "reparagraphing" as Lee Konitz called it, but the stuctures themselves were still locked into regular, even, and divisive phrasing. Gunther Schuller and John Lewis, siding in a way with the classical-music critics of jazz, felt that employing techniques of traditional thematic development and multiple contrasting themes or sections within a composition would take jazz to the next logical step in its evolution and, consequently, resolve one of its significant shortcomings in the eyes of the classical music community.

Another factor in this new merger was, surprisingly, American composers' increasing involvement with atonality and serialism. By the mid-1940s, the American composition community had divided loosely into two basic camps. The first group was the tonalists, those who followed the style of Stravinsky, Aaron Copland, and Bela Bartók. The second group had embraced and developed the atonal and twelve-tone practice of the "Second Viennese School" — Arnold Schoenberg, Anton Webern, and Alban Berg (Peyser 1987). By the 1950s, Schuller was firmly in the second group. The mainstream jazz community had tended to lean more toward the stylistic tendencies of the first group, and was still, in the period after 1945, quite infatuated with the ramifications of French Impressionistic tonal practices such as extended tertian harmony, and tritone and whole-tone usage. However, the approaching jazz practice of polytonal or atonal work, and open or ambiguous formal structures, was leading jazz to be more in line, in a general sense, with post-World-War-II serialism, as well as with formal experimentation in art music. A syncretism seemed to be in order, and once again, the hope of third stram's advocates was to quell accusations about jazz's shortcomings from the art-music community — in this case, that jazz was restricted to employing only conventional tonality or old-fashioned extensions of it.

The objections to Kenton's, Schuller's, and Lewis's ideas of swing, meter, form, and tonality among the jazz orthodoxy are not as much the result of musical conservatism as they might at first seem; they are, rather, the result of a more fundamental clash of a closely held notion of jazz's foundational attributes with third stream's more classical-oriented approach. The concerns tend to focus on: 1) a perceived threat to the maintainance of the characteristic swing feel and pulse, or "groove"; and 2) an unhealthy preoccupation with elaborate writing and formal structures that inhibit creative freedom for the improvising performer (and threaten the ability of a jazz group to maintain a consistent "groove" or swing feel in the music). Improvisational freedom and maintenance of the groove are seen to be paramount to the jazz aesthetic; the fear is that these defining features at the heart of jazz are easily undermined by some of the classical tendencies in third stream discussed above. In short, for the critics of third-stream music the debate is not between new jazz and old jazz; it is between jazz and not-jazz.

In the view of many within the jazz community, jazz begins to suffer and lose its essence without the presence of an overt, constant pulse (DeVeaux 1994). Jazz has never moved so far from the idea of "the groove" that jazz advocates fail to expect it. When jazz pieces cease having a groove, it is considered either a respite between rhythmic sections, an anticipatory effect to build tension (much like a cadenza in a concerto), or just bad jazz. This has been evident in criticism of the Bill Evans Trio with bassist Scott LaFaro, who some critics accused of not swinging. An important and distinctive feature of the Evans trio was the contrapuntal interplay between the bass and piano — a feature that defied the traditional role of "walking bass" as contributing to the projection of a steady pulse and groove. The same was said of the Dave Brubeck Quartet, a group that experimented with compound meters and was one of the most rhythmically explorative jazz groups of the 1950s and 1960s. Brubeck, it is important to note, was a major influence on modern pianists Cecil Taylor and Paul Bley.

To fully realize the gravity of these issues, we have to come to a basic understanding of what creates swing or a groove. Swing is best defined as the superimposition of relaxation over tension. The tension is the insistent, audible, and regular underlying rhythmic pulse. The relaxation is the various contrapuntal interactions against or between that pulse. Scott Joplin and other ragtime pianists certainly realized this basic duality, which is why the piano is the instrument best suited to creating the "ragtime effect" of a syncopated melody over a steady bass. This rhythmic duality was also observed early on by Igor Stravinsky, who said "Which of us, when listening to jazz, has not felt an amusing and almost giddy sensation when a dancer or solo musician persists in marking irregular accentuations but does not succeed in diverting the ear from the regular pulsation beaten out by the percussion?" (Stravinsky 1942, 45). Stravinsky's inference, as I read it, is somewhat condescending: try as they might, he seems to be saying, syncopated melodies in jazz never quite obscure the regular meter. He is obviously comparing the function of syncopation in jazz to what he so successfully achieved in pieces such as *Le Sacre du Printemps*, a monument of rhythmic innovation that does not happen to swing in performance (nor, to be fair, is that the intent). Stravinsky failed to see that syncopation in jazz does not function to obscure the basic pulse; it rather creates a duality, a dialectic. In his *Jazz: Its Evolution and Essence*, André Hodeir accurately assesses the importance of the basic pulse:

> The rhythms of jazz, which are very simple in themselves, have the "giddy" power Stravinsky refers to only when they are set against a steady beat. By destroying the basic pulsation, our composers killed the principle of attraction on which the phenomenon of swing depends. The positive element of an electric current has no power if it is cut off from the negative element, its opposite; and in the same way, a syncopated rhythm becomes insignificant and loses it Dionysian power when cut off from its invaluable auxiliary. (Hodeir 1980, 260–261)

Mere use of syncopation, however, is not enough to create the compelling effect of swing. Another important element of swing is the manner of articulation and accentuation. It is one of the most subtle and elusive of swing elements, much more so than playing syncopated rhythms. This type of playing works at both extremes, sharply articulating selected notes while barely uttering others, referred to in jazz parlance as "ghosted" notes. There is also the use of a generally softer attack of the note, a "doo" rather than "too" articulation that creates a swing sensation. This is the opposite of the crisp, sharp articulation considered desirable in rhythmically active pieces in the European tradition such as, for instance, marches. Articulation was a point of controversy between the hard bop and cool bop aesthetic. The cool school subscribed to the philosophy of a soft timbre and accentuation in order to heighten the effect of asymmetrical phrasing. Streams of eighth notes were played with relatively even emphasis and almost evenly, compared to the 2:1 ratio characteristic of "swing eighths," which accent the upbeat more. In employing European-style trained musicians in the performance of third-stream pieces, the proper articulation necessary for the ensemble to swing has been a particularly difficult to achieve. The nature of bowed string instruments seems particularly susceptible to this kind of rhythmic shortcoming. This single factor probably accounts for the reason so many third-stream pieces are formatted in a concerto-grosso format; the swinging is left to the jazz musicians, while textural filler and the "classical" portions are relegated to the traditionally trained orchestral musicians.

Maintenance of rhythmic momentum and the groove has a decided effect on form. The more expansive developmental practice of Romantic-era composition catered more to use of rubato and less to the custody of rhythmic momentum. The apparent formlessness of rhythm-oriented musics from Africa and India reminds us that elaborate structural form interrupts rhythmic momentum, whereas repetition of shorter strophes contributes to the momentum of the groove. This results in a spiraling rather than circular effect. In other words, the repetition, rather than going nowhere, rolls forward and builds in momentum.

Form is the biggest incentive for the rise of third-stream music and certainly the biggest issue in comparing the two musical traditions of jazz and classical music. It is the aspect many assume classical music has the best control of and that jazz most quaintly tries to imitate. It is important to bear in mind, however, that prescriptive composition and improvisation have two different goals in mind, and imposing the criterion of one on the other is fruitless and self-defeating. Therefore, observations of formal structure are best employed for purposes of stylistic comparison, and not as a means of determining musical superiority.

Classical music uses venerable forms such as the rondo, sonata allegro, fugue, motivic developmental processes, and other structural models and procedures. Developmental elaboration may include elongation or contraction of the prescribed form, disturbing regularity of repetition in the form, such as one gets with theme and variations. This allows for points of great rhythmic repose (rubati, cadenzas, etc.), particularly in the Romantic repertoire, with no particular obligation to maintain a steady tempo since the music is primarily for listening. The dramatic pacing of a prescribed classical piece is determined out of real time, without spontaneity (but with a great deal of contemplation), and is often a logical working out of the thematic, harmonic, rhythmic, and/or formal material. Formal designs do not facilitate spontaneous musical intervention and elaboration; instead, they are more preoccupied with the intricacies of the compositional craft itself.

In the realm of written jazz compositions and arrangements, one traditionally finds the head-choruses-head format and the strophic use of compact forms such as the 12-bar blues, the 32-bar song form, or a through-composed theme usually based on a couple of riffs or a chord cycle. Jazz compositions are lengthened in a number of ways, often through multiple choruses of solo improvisations or written passages for sections of instruments. Longer concert jazz works are often in the form of suites, a collection of short pieces programmatically strung together to create a longer work; a variation on that idea is a single piece with multiple contrasting themes. It is exceedingly rare to find a lengthy jazz work based on a single theme that does not rely on improvisation for most of its elaboration: such a piece, in any case, would miss the improvisational ideal of the jazz aesthetic anyway.

Improvisation is a spontaneous creation in reaction to the musical and environmental situation of the moment. Jazz improvisational form is therefore shaped by emotional decision. A jazz musician draws from a mental lexicon of formulae and assembles an ongoing melody that coincides with the harmonic sequence and the metric pattern, yet (hopefully) creates a satisfying and compelling dramatic event. There is rarely reference to material used earlier in the solo, since the material is created spontaneously and quickly forgotten. The only recurring factor is the repetition of the underlying form of the prescribed composition, the vehicle over which one improvises. (The exception to this is improvisation in the "free jazz" style, which uses no formal underpinning and alters the improvising behavior to some extent.) The design of this improvisitory event changes with each new performance, as the improvisor negotiates between his/her own sense of tension and release and what seems appropriate to the mood of the audience and the fellow players. It is essential that the improvisor be free to react unencumbered to the prescribed piece, the other musicians, and their own muse. Complex, elongated, and unpredictable forms pose a distraction to the improvising musician and are not fertile ground for spontaneous creativity. Indeed, by the late 1950s, a large contingent worked toward abandoning form altogether in order to keep their improvisations as unfettered as possible. This creates the most basic aesthetic clash between classical music and jazz: compositional control versus improvisational freedom.

Jazz improvisation, in the hard bop ideal, flourishes only in the most delicate of situations. The prescribed form provides guideposts and gives the soloist points of measurement where they decide to rephrase, change ideas, or defy. On the other hand, the form must help maintain the momentum of the groove and not impose upon the spontaneous dramatic shape created by the improvising musician. This has resulted in the general use of the 32-bar AABA or AA' form of Tin Pan Alley popular song and the twelve-bar blues form as vehicles for jazz improvisation. Beginning in the 1950s, through-composed chord-cycle pieces approximately sixteen bars in length ("Tune Up," "Pent-Up House," "Giant Steps," etc.) were added to the canon. The strophic repetition of the form both maintains the groove and provides a predictable underpinning for the improvisor. For the listener who is more composition-oriented and oblivious to the process of the improvisation, this practice is formally tedious and simplistic. To the musicians preoccupied with the act of improvisation, the prescribed form is merely a facilitator to spontaneous creativity. When the form-oriented composer attempts to apply a more expansive prescribed form on the improvisor, he imposes sanctions on the improvisor that conflict with his musical ideal. This is one of the reasons that ragtime ultimately died as a vehicle for jazz. As spontaneous improvisation became more of a preoccupation in jazz, the ragtime form proved too lengthy and complex. Being dominantly a written tradition, ragtime did not facilitate improvisation beyond mere embellishment of the prescribed notes. One of the themes, usually the third (in the subdominant key), became the vehicle for solos, repeated until everyone had their fill. Over the course of the 1920s, ragtime gradually fell into disuse in favor of the briefer popular song form.

Here we come to the basic problem in blending the techniques, styles, and aesthetics of two very different musical traditions. We are reminded repeatedly that the employment of elaborate formal design was the primary issue in the rise of third-stream music. But as form becomes more extensive, it also becomes more restrictive to rhythmic momentum (the groove) and the discretion of the improvising soloist to design a spontaneous dramatic shape. Groove and spontaneity are also impeded by the use of classically trained musicians not conversant in the rhythmic subtleties that create a swing feel. Third stream smacked of European art-music elitism, implying that classical music approaches had come to the rescue of jazz, solving a problem that jazz aficionados never thought existed in the first place. The final failure of third stream was its supposed attempt to reach a broader audience. Jazz fans view formal orchestral presentations of jazz as stuffy. Classical audiences view a bopping jazz tenor saxophone soloist standing in the middle of a symphony orchestra as quaint. Even the most sympathetic observer of third stream rarely regards the effort as much more than heartwarming diplomacy between two musical cultures.

In recent years, "third stream" has been redefined by Schuller, his main disciple Ran Blake, and the Third Stream department of the New England Conservatory of Music, the legacy of Schuller's tenure there as president in the 1960s and 70s. Third stream now supposedly encompasses the improvised tradition in combination with world ethnic musics, no longer only the European art-music tradition. Nevertheless, as late as 30 April 1995, Schuller appeared on National Public Radio's news program Weekend Edition Sunday to promote his compact disc *Rush Hour* (Blue Note CDP 7243 8 29269 2 4), a collaborative effort with saxophonist Joe Lovano.

Schuller still expresses the traditional concerns and goals of third stream: formal expansion beyond the head-choruses-head format of many jazz performances, use of traditionally non-jazz instruments, and a tonal vocabulary that moves beyond the thread-bare pentatonic and tetra-chordal language of post-Coltrane. Schuller insists that this project is not simply "third stream thirty-five years later," but an effort to revitalize jazz through new musical resources.

There is one final issue reflected in the third-stream effort, the artistic striving for innovation — for the "new thing." Unfortunately, this is yet another area where third stream failed. It failed because it quickly, artificially, and self-consciously tried to fuse disparate traditions together. Such fusions are not impossible, of course, but they are usually achieved only over a long, natural, and unselfconscious period of syncretism; like a good sauce, flavors must have time to blend. The creators as well as consumers of the new product must have time to acclimate to the new stylistic environment; the product also must be something with which a large group can identify, enough so that the new musical practice moves toward the mainstream of the culture.

In terms of this last criticism — that it never really caught on with a broader public, even within the jazz community — third stream does not deserve exclusive condemnation. Throughout this essay, I have used the term "mainstream" to refer to the large audience for popular music, to the classical and contemporary classical community, and to the bebop and free jazz communities. But in today's musical setting, Arthur C. Danto finds no mainstream at all, "simply confluences of individual tributaries with no mainstream to flow into" (Danto 1989, 794). In the latter half of the twentieth century, we find there is no overwhelming stylistic leader, no standard of innovation, either in classical music, jazz, or popular music. Schuller himself stated this in his keynote address to the 1980 conference of the American Society of University Composers. Third stream obviously has not turned out to be the answer in establishing a new musical tradition or stylistic offspring. As composer Larry Austin once put it, third-stream music is a mule. It cannot replicate itself; one is forced to go back to the horse and donkey each time and start over. Third stream does, however, celebrate the spirit of diversity in American music, and even its harshest critics would acknowledge that, at its best, third-stream music at least exhibits the exploratory and innovative tendencies that are the hallmark of true art.

References

Blesh, Rudi, and Harriet Janis. 1950. *They All Played Ragtime*. New York: Oak Publications.

Brown, Robert Loran, Jr. 1974. *A Study of Influences From Euro-American Art Music On Certain Types of Jazz With Analyses and Recital of Selected Demonstrative*. Ph.D. dissertation, Columbia University.

Bürger, Peter. 1984. *The Theory of the Avant-Garde*. Minneapolis: University of Minnesota Press.

Cerulli, Dom. 1961. "Liner notes to Eddie Sauter and Stan Getz", *Focus* Verve, V6-8412.

Danto, Arthur C. 1989. "Women and Mainstream Art". *Nation* (25 December): 794–798.

Daryll, Ted. 1992. "Liner notes to Stan Kenton", *Retrospective*, Capitol CDP7 97350 2.

DeVeaux, Scott. 1994. The Africa Connection. *Jazz Player Magazine* 1/2: 6–10.

Friedwald, Will. 1991. Liner notes to *Stan Kenton: The Complete Capitol Recordings of the Holman and Russo Charts*, Mosaic MD4-136.

Hasse, John, ed. 1985. *Ragtime: Its History, Composers, and Music*. New York: Schirmer Books.

Hentoff, Nat. 1952. "Jazz Isn't Meant to Continue as Dance Music, Says Kenton". *Downbeat* 19/17 (27 August): 6–9.

Hodeir, André. 1962. *Toward Jazz*, rev. ed. New York: Grove Press.

Hodeir, André. 1980. *Jazz: Its Evolution and Essence*, rev. ed. New York: Grove Press.

Kenton, Stan. 1951. "Liner notes to *The City of Glass/This Modern World*". Creative World Records ST 1006.

Levant, Oscar. 1950. *A Smattering of Ignorance*. New York: Doubleday, Doran and Co.

Litweiler, John. 1992. *Ornette Coleman: A Harmolodic Life*. New York: Morrow Books.

Peyser, Joan. 1987. *Bernstein: A Biography*. New York: Beech Tree Books.

Radano, Ronald M. 1993. *New Musical Figurations*. Chicago: University of Chicago Press.

Schuller, Gunther. 1986a. "Third Stream", in *The New Grove Dictionary of American Music*, ed. H. Wiley Hitchcock and Stanley Sadie. New York: Grove's Dictionaries of Music.

Schuller, Gunther. 1986b. *Musings: The Musical Worlds of Gunther Schuller*. New York: Oxford University Press.

Schuller, Gunther. 1987. "Editorial preface to George Russell's 'All About Rosie'". Newton Centre, Mass.: Margun Music.

Stravinsky, Igor. 1942. *The Poetics of Music in the Form of Six Lessons*. Trans. Arthur Knodel and Ingolf Dahl. Cambridge, Mass.: Harvard University Press.

Stuessy, Clarence Joseph. 1977. *The Confluence of Jazz and Classical Music From 1950–1970*. Ph.D. dissertation, The University of Rochester, Eastman School of Music.

Contemporary Music Review
2000, Vol. 19, Part 1, pp. 89–111
Reprints available directly from the publisher
Photocopying permitted by license only

Into the Ivory Tower: Vernacular Music and the American Academy

Austin B. Caswell and Christopher Smith

This paper examines the historical methods and motives for the incorporation of select vernacular music idioms into the American university system. We look at the history of four music genres — choral music, bands, piano music, and jazz — whose cultural status has been debated and manipulated in order to render them acceptable pedagogical topics. Drawing on the extensive literature which accompanied these debates, we present a model for the dualistic philosophical debate between utilitarian and aestheticist perspectives, and suggest that the incorporation of vernacular idioms into university curricula consistently reflects this debate. Finally, we show that the value and meaning of vernacular musics have been significant philosophical issues throughout the history of American university education.

KEYWORDS: Vernacular music; social context; social function; musical behavior; musical artifacts; utilitarian philosophy; aestheticist philosophy; jazz; band music; choral music; solo piano music

Introduction

This paper examines the historical methods and motives for the incorporation of select vernacular music idioms into the American university system. We look at the history of four music genres — choral music, bands, piano music, and jazz — whose cultural status has been debated and manipulated in order to render them acceptable pedagogical topics. Drawing on the extensive literature which accompanied these debates, we show that the value and meaning of vernacular musics have been significant philosophical issues throughout the history of American university education.

American educational philosophies have often attempted to hierarchize music genres: to assign idioms cultural value, in order to place them in a schematized ranking of greater or lesser relative worth. We suggest that this hierarchizing impulse reflects a culture-wide debate between what may be termed utilitarian versus aestheticist philosophies; with music idioms, the "utilitarian" proof of value has depended upon demonstrating an idiom's usefulness, social or monetary value, applicability, etc., whereas the "aestheticist" proof argues for a specific idiom's inhering, immanent value, independent of its practical usefulness.

The debate's nature, topics and terminology recur in a variety of historical and contextual cases. Moreover, the evidence proves to be both functional and reflective: the literature simultaneously displays and enacts the manipulation and reassessment of a particular genre's status. Therefore, we can attempt to show not only what happened, but also why.

Defining "Utilitarian" and "Aestheticist"

The hierarchical debate of utilitarian versus aestheticist perspectives is too complex and rich a topic to permit a comprehensive examination here, but certain factors are essential to our argument. First, that this debate is central to American cultural identity is revealed by the consistency with which it has been argued: specifically, cultural arbiters have fought recurrent polemical battles over the value of various music idioms in education. In addition, the debate is cyclic: similar questions are raised and philosophies espoused at different historical periods and in support of different music genres, yet with similar patterns, goals, and results.

Second, since the beginning of European culture in the New World, a strong current of self-conscious comparison to the Old World has made the arts a fundamental tool for creating, delineating, and sharply distinguishing American identity. The expressive arts are a central means by which Americans have "told ourselves about ourselves." Music, as ratified in pedagogy, has repeatedly been employed as a weapon in the psychosocial battle for the power to articulate American cultural aspirations.

Third, negotiation of genres' hierarchical status has often been accomplished through what may be termed a "quantifying impulse." Cultural critics have attempted to establish the pre-eminent status of a music genre by superimposing objective language, associations, and assessments on subjective phenomena.[1] Having done so, they were enabled to argue for a hierarchical system of value: if one genre's total "quantified value" exceeded another's, then the first could be placed higher in the cultural hierarchy.

In the case of vernacular genres — those which had their foundation in musical life outside the academy or other formalized cultural institutions — such value was most often assessed in utilitarian terms: a genre was argued to be worthwhile because it gave pleasure, directed human energy into manageable channels, stirred patriotic or humanitarian impulses, etc. Conversely, genres seeking inclusion in the academy most often were evaluated in aestheticist terms: through claims of their inhering, immanent value. Such aestheticist value precluded the necessity of showing utilitarian applications.

A dualistic academic perspective on these two viewpoints led to presumptions that vernacular genres were inferior, specifically because of their utilitarian connotations. Hence, advocates for these genres' entrance into academia were forced to redefine and recontextualize them, in order to excise their inadmissible utilitarian associations.

The means by which genres were quantified and hierarchized were a direct outgrowth of an American desire to reify "cultural objects" over "cultural behaviors." Cultural arbiters wanted works and institutions ("objects") which were on a par with Europe's, but also wished to sanitize these objects of inacceptable contextual and behavioral associations. Thus it became necessary to find strategies that permitted simultaneous assignment of high value to the objects themselves, and the excision of the contexts and behaviors from which they arose.[2]

Such a model enacts dualistic constructions of cultural value. It permits separation of the object's creator, who engages in a constructive process, and its assessor, whose involvement is evaluative and contemplative. The constructive contribution is minimized, the evaluative stance is reified, and an object acquires cultural value only after it has been evaluated by an expert critic. The technical, psychological and communicative processes create the art form, but because resistant to traditional critical or analytical processes, they are made secondary to the more receptive, and thus fetishized, score, text, or recorded performance. "Music" becomes a canonic collection of objects, not a communicative repertoire of behaviors.

Choral Music

Building a niche for choral music in American musical academia was an easy task in some ways, hard in others. Americans of all classes had long had comfortable familiarity with a wide variety of choral music traditions, all of which had an advantage over solo instrumental music; they reflected American democratic ideologies which privileged the submission of the individual to a group identity. But almost all had drawbacks of original context. What was needed was a body of music that could be stripped of its original contextual definition — stripped of its nature as a cultural signifier for those who originally sang it and listened to it — and ascribed value as "great music" — an appropriate musical diet for young people being trained as leaders of society.

For example, the tradition of the *Männerchor* — German immigrant men's choruses whose singing was a palpable declaration of cultural identity — was too closely associated with that function and that cultural group to serve academia; audiences would have difficulty defining such a repertoire as "great music." The same would apply to the music of the college glee club. Although already part of the culture of the campus, it defined its singers and audiences in the wrong way: carefree adolescents rejecting the strictures of maturity. Choral music from religious worship was acceptable only to the degree that its religious practice was aesthetically productive, i.e., able to produce "great music." Thus, religions of European provenance and some antiquity (e.g., Renaissance Catholicism, English Anglicanism, and German Lutheranism) might make contributions acceptable to academia's requirements, but American Fundamentalism certainly could not.

The English-language oratorio proved a good candidate. It had already acquired an elitist aesthetic — music performed by amateurs of the upper classes for audiences of their peers to demonstrate sensitivity to "great music," and separation from the "insensitive" classes.[3] The performance traditions of oratorio societies offered visual reinforcements that appealed to academia's search for badges of respectability: concerts presented in formal dress before audiences listening in respectful silence. Its mode of presentation served the elitist image academia wished to portray, while its music — Handel and his stylistic descendants — already enjoyed acceptance as "great music" in the eyes of European critics.[4]

The sacred music of J. S. Bach entered the academic repertory not as music practiced by German Lutheran immigrants, but as the devout utterance of the composer already designated by European scholars as the pinnacle of Western music culture; thus it could be shorn of its German vernacular identity and presented as music whose greatness spoke to audiences regardless of their cultural origins. By appropriating artifacts whose "greatness" was already unassailable and performance behaviors safely associated with elitism, American musical academics built a good case for the academic appropriateness of choral performance. Between the two World Wars, a movement to further elevate academic choral performance emerged. The a cappella movement sought to spiritualize choral singing by eliminating the secular associations of instrumental accompaniment, positing that unaccompanied music was not only more difficult to sing, but more difficult to compose, since it called on the composer to communicate his ideas without the assistance of instruments.[5] Thus we witness the decontextualization of the Catholic motet and mass as musical liturgies of the Roman Catholic Church and their recontextualization as great music performed by American liberal arts college students manifesting their sensitivity to great music by substituting devotion to the musical work for devotion to God. The result appealed not only through its appropriation of artifacts of certifiable quality, but also as behavior demonstrating the American ideal of democracy: the untrained amateur achieving something possible only through voluntary contribution to the group and submission of self to it.

The most striking example of choral music recontextualized by academe is provided by Robert Shaw, who built his career on reintroducing academia's definition of choral music into public (i.e., non-academic) musical life. Shaw is thus the final arc in the circle in which the academy first took choral music from its utilitarian position in the community, aestheticized it to serve the academy's purposes, and then reintroduced it into the non-academic community in a new definition. But though the circle is complete, we must note that the journey has thoroughly transformed the music; it is no longer the same when it returns to the community as it was when taken from it. Performed in concert by a meticulously rehearsed ensemble of trained singers, the sentimental ballad of the *Männerchor* is no longer a way for the immigrant community to proclaim its identity; the Black spiritual is no longer an outcry of an enslaved race, and the Handel oratorio no longer an exercise in English mercantile piety. Nor are they vehicles for college students to demonstrate what the study of music can do for them. They have become something else: "significant" works in a choral canon articulated by music academics.

Having transformed the public choral concerts from utilitarian to aesthetic events by appropriating the academic definition, Shaw was able to reclaim the repertory earlier dismissed as trivial. Convincing audiences that his choirs could achieve an exalted state by strenuous effort,[6] Shaw made the radical step of asserting that this athletic asceticism made any repertory acceptable. Thus, the very college songs, vaudeville numbers, and folk tunes earlier rejected by the academy were admitted to the company of Bach, Handel, and Palestrina by virtue not of inherent aesthetic value, but through appropriate musical devotion on the part of their performers.

Shaw's recipe satisfies many needs of American culture: in positioning the aesthetic paradigm of choral excellence (and rendering the repertory's original contextuality irrelevant) Shaw establishes that college singers are superior to the repertory's original performers; i.e., musically more skilled and aesthetically more sensitive than Black slaves, Lutheran choirboys, and English merchants. This assertion appeals strongly to America's musical morality: arguing that voices drawn from a democratic society can, through hard work and dedication, perform any music better than its original performers, thus demonstrating democracy's musical, as well as political, superiority.

The route taken by academic choral music is a curious one. Academia, if convinced a repertory has the potential to serve the academic aesthetic, appropriates it and strips it of its original function. Having "purified" (and decontextualized) the repertory, musical academia can aestheticize it in whatever way best serves, making a niche for the genre in the canon of "great works."

But this raises some concerns. As Alasdair MacIntyre puts it:

> When the Catholic mass becomes a genre available for concert performance by Protestants, when we listen to the scripture because of what Bach wrote rather than because of what St. Matthew wrote, then sacred links with belief have been broken . . . a traditional distinction between the religious and the aesthetic has been blurred. (MacIntyre, 1981)

MacIntyre speaks from a concern for the integrity of religion, but the same concern could be voiced for the integrity of music. The academy's alteration of choral music from utilitarian statements of cultural identity to de-contextualized art works is clearly a distortion of the original intent. This loss of processual/contextual function and original communicative intent means a repertoire becomes a way for musicians to talk to themselves rather than to others.

Yet in another sense, academia is not destroying choral singing's original function of cultural identification but rather substituting a new one. Demonstrating that young, untrained amateurs from a democratic society can surpass the efforts of European conservatory-trained professionals is itself a utilitarian statement of cultural identity.[7] This has been accepted as a role uniquely appropriate to choral music because the chorus symbolizes the massed utterance of democratic masses using their natural "instruments" to utter truths associated with the convictions of the singers themselves.

Band Music

The history of American band music provides an opportunity to trace the transformation of a genre's definition from utilitarian to aestheticist. Primary sources make it clear that band music's associations with functional, communal, and non-academic music-making were deemed inappropriate for inclusion in university curricula. As a result, band leaders, teachers, and other advocates consciously chose to recontextualize and redefine "what band music was" in order to excise inappropriate associations and raise the genre's status. This was accomplished by transforming both the external context in which band music was presented, and the internal specifics which defined it.

Unlike the soloistic genres, where the legitimizing goal was excision of individualist behavior, communal band music required reconstruction of context and content. The "business men who were the band men" of the 1880s, who had performed at dances and breweries for smokes and drinks, did not fit the desired stereotype of the clean-cut college boys whose moral and intellectual fibre was to be shaped by the university experience; nor did their music.[8] A village brass band of amateurs who met in order to play polkas at a political rally was a participatory, communal, and socially relevant experience, but it was also one whose class and behavioral connotations were unacceptable to academia. In fact, all manner of vernacular music-making went on in community contexts; it was a "problem" only insofar as arbiters of taste believed that other music had greater merit and should supplant it.[9]

The public roots of the band movement have been traced as far back as fife-and-drum ensembles of the Revolution, and to the avocational town and village bands of the 19th century. However, prior to the Civil War, formalized group *instruction* in music practice had been limited to methods and techniques for choral singing,[10] and had not extended to instrumental or ensemble training. The social and economic upheaval that surrounded and followed the Civil War provided stimulus for change in music education (Wagner 1989).[11]

Manuals published during Reconstruction attempted to provide under one cover all the instruction necessary for a bandleader to found, recruit, and direct such musical ensembles. These manuals make it clear that, in 1888, a gap already existed between utility and aesthetics, between practice and pedagogy:

The men who know practically how to prepare Band music, and are actually engaged in that work, are most all Germans, and though thoroughly familiar with the whole process, are yet incapable of writing a book of instruction on the subject in English, while on the other hand, the men who do attempt to write such books, are for the most part profound English and American theorists who can tell all about Symphonies, Sonatas, etc., but *not one in ten of whom could arrange a Brass Band Polka in a proper and effective manner to save his life*, not because he would be deficient in musical knowledge, but *because these scientific gentlemen have no practical acquaintance* with the band instruments and the manner of writing for them. (Quoted in Wagner 1989; emphasis added)

Even before the War, band-training in primary education exhibits a utilitarian orientation;[12] Kapfer refers to a

pattern of introducing and justifying music in the public school on practical grounds, and using music on occasion for utilitarian purposes . . . The bands apparently were used in observances of holidays and special occasions as a means of generating school spirit, patriotic fervor, and well-disciplined behavior among students . . . [and] to attract favorable attention among parents and other citizens to the *entire course of instruction*. (Kapfer 1968; emphasis added)

While some "school authorities decried the band and class (music) lessons as unorthodox" (Historian 1950), it was generally and widely believed that primary school bands served a valid functional purpose, providing a useful means of raising a school's funds and its visibility in the community, and of channeling young people's energies. However, there was no implication that practical music education and skills might be philosophically relevant to post-primary or non-vocational academia.

The advocates of band music's inclusion in university curricula acted as self-conscious, historicizing assessors of cultural values, employing quantitative claims of newness and size to extrapolate qualitative hierarchical evaluations. One specific strategy, the "great-man" paradigm, is involved most blatantly and extensively in biographies of Albert Austin Harding. Trained as a professional musician, Harding took over the fledgling band program at the University of Illinois in 1905 and held that post until 1948. During Harding's tenure, which encompassed the crucial period of the World Wars (1914–45), he transformed the context, behaviors and definition of bands and band music. Like Robert Shaw in choral music and Paul Whiteman in jazz, Harding was described as a "great man" who had led a formerly disreputable genre out of the utilitarian, proletariat shadows into the Apollonian sunlight of academic aesthetics.

In addition to providing a handy historical framework, the great-man paradigm was a convenient tool for legitimizing a genre by association. Because Harding was a "leader (and) influential figure" who "set the tone which determine(d) the course of future development ," his area of specialization could also be presented as reputable, credible, and susceptible of greatness.

Harding's own subtle understanding of social and cultural semiotics is revealed by the ways in which he tailored his own rhetoric. For community bands, he invoked legitimacy by analogous association with beloved cultural institutions: "Pride and loyalty are the primary requisites for establishing and maintaining a good baseball team . . . or band in a community" (Harding 1915), and by arguments for their utilitarian value:

The band is . . . the most useful musical body in the community; in fact, it is almost indispensable . . . The band will exercise a certain influence upon each individual in the town. Why should not that influence be directed toward the development of public taste in music? (Harding 1915)

In contrast, when addressing the cultural arbiters who shaped university curricula, he altered his rhetoric: emphasizing the newness, uniqueness, and innovation of the repertoires programmed, and explicitly linking the bands' self-evaluation and presentation with that of the university itself (Weber 1967). As historians legitimized band music by association with

Harding the "great man," Harding himself further legitimized the music's attributed goals by associating them with the abstract ideals of the university and by manipulating internal style characteristics. Such "redefinition" would have crucial stylistic impact on the genre.

First, he expanded the basic instrumentation of the military marching band to include instruments explicitly associated with the symphonic orchestra — woodwinds, strings, and orchestral percussion (Weber 1967) — whose specific class and gender associations were appropriated for legitimizing effect.[13]

Second, he encouraged and extensively engaged in transcription, believing that "lack of a serious literature of significant proportions ha[d] been one of the major handicaps of the concert band" (Weber 1967). As revaluative tools he invoked both the European repertoires' hierarchical status and the massive forces necessary to perform them, equating "bigger with better" and ranking "European as best":

Great pride is taken in the quality of the band's programs. Besides all of the standard overtures and selections, Tschaikowsky symphonies, Wagnerian music-dramas and the Puccini operas are represented on its programs. Last spring the mighty '1812' Overture was given by the massed bands of 180 players, augmented by the university organ. (Harding 1915)

Finally A. A. Harding, like the apologists for ragtime and choral music, on occasion preached a utilitarian rationale in support of an aestheticist objective:

Grown-up people are like children in the matter of musical taste, you must bribe them with sweets to get them to take wholesome food ... After all, the ultimate conclusion is that *the public must be educated against its will.* You must tempt the people to come to hear the things they like; then make them sit through the things they will understand when they have heard them enough. That is the band's mission. (Harding 1915; emphasis added.)

These strategies were not problematic in and of themselves, but became so because hierarchizing apologists accepted them uncritically. While this facilitated band music winning a place in the academic food-chain, it also constructed a dualistic, comparative model, one which awarded hierarchical value to objects and genres only by devaluing processes and other genres. These tendencies privileged one sub-style over another.

The status of band departments within the academic community to which they have finally been admitted is still linked to old functional assessments (Boyd 1952) and to presumptions about the characteristic personalities attributed to practitioners of certain genres (Scott 1964). Old hierarchical, classist and gendered presumptions die hard,[14] even in the case of genres which appear to have reconciled utilitarian and aestheticist roles.[15] Most recently, attempts have been made to justify the study of band music and band music history as a branch of the historical performance movement (Borowicz 1990 and Marquis 1971).

The wheel has come full circle: from its origins as a utilitarian, functional, and communal activity, through redefinition and recontextualization band music has won a place of value in conservatory budgets and university curricula. Yet now, like other genres whose vernacular roots were excised in the process of self-assimilation, band music must battle to "prove" the broader functional relevance which at one time in our history was its unacceptable, yet most potent, cultural attribute.

Solo Piano Music

As American colleges and universities embraced music in the late nineteenth century, they first admitted to credit-bearing status courses claiming intellectual content by association with established disciplines. Music history was "scholarly" by definition, composition was linked to rhetoric, and music appreciation to English literature. Instrumental performance, however, had a more difficult row to hoe because it was associated with activities difficult to label as intellectual pursuits. Many policy-makers were convinced that training for a performing career was not appropriate to the goals of higher education and was best left to the conservatory or to the apprenticeship system.

In the case of piano instruction, the dilemma of repertory was an added impediment. Although the enshrinement of J. S. Bach as the greatest of all composers had ensured a place for the analytical/historical study of his keyboard scores, it was felt that they served the pianist well only as etudes and, because of high "scholarly" content, could not appeal to a concert audience. The domestic repertoire of parlor music was felt inappropriate for the opposite reason; it was seen as too utilitarian and too feminine[16] to bear serious study and, since functionally entertaining for the family circle, of no substance meriting academic credit. In short, the only repertoire available to be considered for college curricula was that of the concert virtuoso; it was the only one having the requisite intellectual, technical, and affective challenges. It had semiotic baggage, however, that posed problems.

The nineteenth-century virtuoso pianist was as well-known on this continent as in Europe; his concerts were just as popular, as commercially oriented, and as sensually presented as were those of European virtuosos. American music educators were well aware of the idolatry and wordless sensual discourse associated with virtuoso pianism.[17] An account of Franz Liszt's public reception will remind us of this discourse and serve as a counter-balance to the entrenched academic perspective concentrating on his compositions and overlooking his persona.

Liszt . . . is an amiable fiend who treats his mistress — the piano — now tenderly, now tyrannically, devours her with kisses, lacerates her with lustful bites, embraces her, caresses her, sulks with her, scolds her, rebukes her, grabs her by the hair, clasps her then all the more delicately, more affectionately, more passionately, more flamingly, more meltingly; exults with her to the heavens, soars with her through all the skies and finally settles down with her in a vale of flowers covered by a canopy of stars . . . After the concert Liszt stands there like a victor on the battlefield, like a hero at a tournament. Daunted pianos lie around him; torn strings wave like flags of truce; frightened instruments flee into distant corners; the listeners look at each other as after a cataclysm of nature that has just passed by, as after a storm out of a clear sky, as after thunder and lightning, mingled with a rain of flowers and a snow of petals and a shimmering rainbow; and he stands there leaning melancholically on his chair, smiling strangely, like an exclamation point after the outbreak of general admiration. Thus is Franz Liszt. (Quoted from Saphir in Loesser 1954)

The virtuoso pianist's reception was not based on musical parameters alone; on the contrary, his audiences were drawn by a compelling public persona. It is also clear that concerts did not focus on the virtuoso as composer of great works. The focus was rather upon the musician as performer — a performer of self. In Liszt's case — and in many others — the incandescent power of the performer's persona was seen as potentially dangerous to public order and morality because of the sexual analogues perceived in the dialogue between male concert hero and young female listener.

The social power of this discourse posed a problem for the curriculum in piano instruction. No academic institution could risk embracing a body of music whose intent was to set up a sensual dialogue between the performer and his listeners, especially when most of those listeners were respectable young women inexperienced in the world of the emotions.[18] The dilemma was how to clean up this music — to excise its original ethos of the sensual performance of the virtuoso's persona and substitute an ethos of inherent compositional value — in short, how to remove the original context of performance event and redefine the music as great work.

Part of the solution was to divorce the composition from its original significance as personal communication for either the virtuoso performer in concert or the student performer in academia. The original performer was re-cast as a "great composer," the student performer was seen as an investigative interpreter whose job was to communicate, not herself, but the great composer's intentions. This was made explicit in program notes or introductory commentary that assiduously avoided discussion of sensual communication, concentrating instead on compositional values inhering in the work itself.

But how to define the new aesthetic of the art-work to supplant that of the performer? Harlow Gale presents two sets of criteria to be considered by the shapers of music curricula. The first he labels unworthy of respect, the second as lofty and noble:

"A table of psychological aesthetic values" (Gale 1922).

"unworthy"

>>> decoration, embellishment
>>> accomplishment, success
>>> imitation, custom, propriety
>>> novelty, curiosity, excitement
>>> admiration, praise,
>>> beating (sic), display
>>> jealousy, passion, revenge

"worthy"

>>> nobility, grandeur, peace
>>> purity, serenity, genuineness
>>> ethical struggle, self-control, victory, grace, sweetness, loveliness
>>> love, ecstacy, longing, dreamy sadness
>>> friendship, sympathy, hope
>>> strength, joy, gladness

Urging that music in the academy establish itself by aiming at the "worthy" values, he explains,

When, now, one comes to compare the teaching of music with the other arts, as literature, e.g., it is distressing to see how the lower aesthetic values preponderate. This condition is due to the teachers of music having learned an instrument rather than the literature of music. . . .

Such musicians are on the literary plane of elocutionists, displaying themselves and their organs, rather than the higher values of art works. Occasionally, of course, the average music teacher will chance to play a Bach fugue, a Beethoven sonata, a Schubert impromptu, a Chopin waltz, a Schumann Träumerei, or a Brahms intermezzo; but this is usually because he was taught a stray art-work amid the customary round of studies and display pieces. . . .

How many pianists have sat down in the calm hour and lived themselves into the some fifty classic piano sonatas, into the art-waltzes from Schubert to Brahms, into the tone-poems from Chopin's preludes and Schumann's Carnaval to Liszt's Swiss and Italian Pilgrimage Annals? (Gale 1922)

Gale proposes the only way to find the "higher values" in music is to divorce oneself from the aesthetic of the performer and concentrate on values inherent in the composition itself — values that presumably inhere even after the music's recontextualization. It is worth noting that Gale believes a canon of "great works" necessary for this pursuit; one cannot find "higher values" in music that has no hierarchy of value. Gale's academic recontextualization requires not only a redefinition of the journey, but also provides a road map of the route.

In his trashing of the aesthetic of the virtuoso performer, Gale goes so far as to decry the concerto as deficient in higher aesthetic values:

> How distressing to see college senior women struggling to get in all the notes of a Schütt, Saint-Saëns, or Tschaikowsky concerto, with no idea of *their mediocre art-value*. Concertos on the whole, except as orchestral works, do not compare with our heritage of sonatas, and they should have little place in the piano and violin literature of amateurs. (Gale 1922; emphasis added)

Gale reveals his adherence to the liberal-arts model by aiming his music curriculum at listeners and sensitive amateur players rather than "less sensitive" professional performers.

> When, now, one comes to reflect how more of the higher art elements can be taught in music, let, first of all, a more distinct line be recognized between making professional performers, as soloists, orchestral players and opera singers, on the one hand, and, on the other hand, the teaching of music culturally as one of the arts . . . Then, with *display* and *accomplishment*, the bane of all music, discouraged or eliminated . . . the cultural study of musical art should start with a pure and distinct standard, as in literature, at the top of our educational system. (Gale 1922; emphasis added)

It becomes clear that Gale's recipe for the inclusion of music as a respected part of the curricula of higher education is to pare away the original aesthetic of performance to reveal the work's kernel of immanent value, and to aim this recontextualized construct at the cultivated amateur who uses music not for utilitarian entertainment but to ascend to the higher aesthetic plane of truth. Gale even recommends communication with musical masterpieces not through public performance, but by reading the score in the privacy of the home. "Then, and not till then, do the classics become our real friends and inspirations to everything loveliest and best in this world" (Gale 1922). Gale's positing of silent, private score study as the highest form of musical contemplation represents the ultimate in defensive excision of subjective performance in favor of text-fetishizing "ultimate meaning." This separation of score-as-object from performance as process represents the final step of the journey of decontextualization.

By mid-century, Paul Henry Lang could write in support of music as an academic study by referring to the "canon of great works" aesthetic as a given.[19] Decrying "background" listening, Lang relies on the image of the serious listener trained to focus on the essence of compositional greatness.

Listening to music casually, with the mind tired or engaged in some other activity, or while partaking of a meal, seldom leads to the level of serious art. A person so listening will be a mere consumer, an uncritical one, unless he is enlightened and guided. (Lang 1949)

Implicit in Lang's call is the elitist positioning of the evaluative listener above the constructivist performer. He decries the dominance of music department faculties by "mere practitioners" and the absence of "men who are of the same cultural denomination as their colleagues in the humanities" (Lang 1949), asserting that

While it is patently desirable, even mandatory, to have good artists and practical musicians on the staff of a music department . . . by placing the emphasis on the practical aspects of music the ideal of a liberal education is distorted. (Lang 1949)

Lang holds that the elevation of music study to a position parallel with the other arts is to be accomplished by appointing scholars who can instill a consciousness of historically informed musical style, and by focussing on the critical listener rather than on the performing musician.

It is a fallacy often encountered among professional musicians that music cannot be taught to the non-professional liberal arts student. On the contrary, one of the most important tasks of the college is to teach music to this type of student. (Lang 1949)

Lang's position reflects the consensus arrived at by American musical academia by mid-century: if music is to be included in higher education it must clothe itself in robes suitably humanistic and evaluative. Moreover, it must address itself in the language of the listener — a position requiring a recontextualizing by substituting the fetishizing aesthetic of artifacts for the behavioral discourse of the performer.

Jazz Music: Context, Values and Power

They are blind to the truth who suppose that ragtime is usurping a place in the popular mind and soul which would otherwise be occupied by something which is "good," or who imagine that popular music is responsible for the deterioration of taste, manners and morals . . . "The people" have created their popular music precisely to their need and their taste. As to its having a deteriorating effect on them . . . such a claim is absurd in view of the fact that it is not the music which make the people, but the people who make the music to suit them. (Farwell 1912)

Recontextualization plays a central and in some ways similar role in the historical assimilation of band music and of jazz. Both genres came from localized, utilitarian, and ethnically, socially, or economically specific contexts, and in both cases contextual associations were carefully pared away in order to legitimate the genre's inclusion in curricula. However, other aspects differ: even more than band music, jazz was associated with disreputable performance contexts and social behaviors. The bar-room and brothel origins of ragtime, the "jungle music" Duke Ellington's orchestra played for floor shows at the Cotton Club, the perceived-to-be-lascivious dance movements of the Charleston and Lindy Hop, the mock-ed or vilified personal habits of the beboppers, the radical politics of the late-1960s free players; all carried associations which confronted the university's elitist, intellectual, and socially, racially, or gender-exclusive tendencies.

In *this* respect, the assimilation of jazz shares similarities with the his-torical case of the solo piano repertoire. Both genres were instrumental, virtuosic, and individualist in focus; both repertoires carried indesirable behavioral associations. So, as with piano repertoire, the assimilative goal became excision of jazz's individualist behaviors no less than contextual associations. This excision was accomplished through selective de-emphasis of the music's original practice, practitioners, behaviors, and social con-text. As a result, the evaluative impulse shifted toward an emphasis on a) great repertories; b) great composers and practitioners; and c) explicit canonizing impulses.[20]

In the earliest public debates over the meaning and value of jazz to American society, the terms were essentially functionalist:[21] both detrac-tors and advocates argued the music's utilitarian social impact, not its inherent aesthetic value. However, the debate early took on "extramusi-cal ideological aspects" (McCarrell 1973) which cited the ethical, moral and social impact of African-American popular idioms.[22]

By the 1920s the popularity of New Orleans-style small group jazz led the *Etude*, a high-profile public forum for musicians, critics, and informed connoisseurs, to dedicate a special issue in 1924 to the question "Where is jazz leading America?" The unsigned Editorial introduction demands hierarchical "transmogrification"[23] before the genre can be per-mitted entrance to the explicitly Germanic canon of great music: "The *Etude* has no illusions on Jazz... In its original form it has no place in musical education and deserves none. It will have to be transmogrified many times before it can present its credentials for the Walhall of music" (*Etude* 1924).

In a 1929 *Musical Quarterly* article, titled "Jazz: Debit and Credit," a pair of self-contradictory fiscal and scientific metaphors are invoked to attach quantified value to qualitative, subjected phenomenon (Laubenstein 1929). The author piles a quasi-scientific metaphor atop the title's fiscal one, offering the approximate equation "jazz [is equivalent to] innovation [which is equivalent to] science [and is therefore] Good."[24] Yet finally, in a contradictory mixing of his own metaphors, he assesses the value of jazz in the "debit," arguing that an alleged "experimental" tendency[25] makes jazz inferior to the more "vital" aestheticism of the European tradition.

Not only opponents but also advocates of jazz attempted to manipulate its legitimacy through quantifying impulses: a 1917 article in *Current Opinion* observes that those arbiters of musical taste who disdain a music which sells "at least 50,000,000 copies of popular music yearly" are blind to the fiscal, hence social, relevance of the idiom in question.[26]

At the same time, as early as 1917, aestheticist advocates asked whether "ragtime (might) save the soul of the Native American composer" (*Current Opinion* 1917); that is, whether the African-American idiom might, as Dvořák had argued, be one building block for a great American concert music. These advocates also recognized that a musical ideology which inflated the value of European genres at the expense of native American ones[27] revealed what Wheaton would later call "our inferiority complex about our own culture" (Wheaton 1970): "Here we have in America something really vital in music [e.g., jazz]. It is right before you, yet you pass it by in lofty scorn" (*Current Opinion* 1920).

The university history of jazz pedagogy (that is, teaching the theory, practice, and technical skills required to perform in the idiom) really begins with the period immediately following World War II. Prior to that time, most working jazz musicians had acquired their skills in non-academic settings: jam sessions and regional, youth, or amateur bands. Such vernacular apprenticeship was appropriate and effective at training practitioners in both the musical and the fiscal, logistical and inter-personal skills required by travelling professionals. Jazz musicians from Louis Armstrong in the teens to the Marsalis brothers in the 1970s received crucial mentoring and skills training in primary or secondary school situations, but such training did not make its way upward into the university curriculum until after 1945.

Post-War social, financial, and educational upheaval had a profound impact on university music teaching. With the death of the touring big bands, and the localization and downsizing of jazz performance (from big bands in dance halls to small groups in small clubs), access to "on-the-job" training was severely curtailed.[28] Moreover, there was a reinfusion into the population of returning veterans, many of whom received musical training while in service, and access to the G. I. Bill after demobil-ization. The result was an explosion of interest in university jazz training, particularly in West Coast colleges (Wheaton 1970).

From 1945 onward, and even before, advocates for university jazz stud-ies employed legitimizing tactics of recontextualization and redefinition. In some cases, they did so even with an awareness of that which was lost, including original context, social and behavioral function, and vernacular meaning. Some illustrative examples of such efforts include:

1) Paul Whiteman and George Gershwin's collaboration on "Rhapsody in Blue," which had made an early attempt to legitimize the African-American musical idiom by associating it with European formal structures;

2) The sharp legitimizing insight which caused Charlie Parker, Dizzy Gillespie, Thelonious Monk, and numerous later jazz historians to present bebop (c. 1945) as the moment at which jazz became an "art music" — what Horowitz called "bop's self-consciously abstruse, artistic, aestheticist aspirations" (Horowitz 1975);

3) The efforts of bandleader Stan Kenton, a mentor to the seminal jazz program at North Texas State, who touted "orchestral jazz" as a legitimizing idiom and a standard of complex and desirable sophistication; and

4) The academic career of the brilliant composer and pedagogue David Baker, who codified a classroom method at Indiana University which effectively taught, but also canonized, one individual's interpretation of the language and techniques of bebop as jazz's "common-practice period."

Music, Morality, Race, Class, and Gender

In a 1912 article, Arthur Farwell asked whether ragtime[29] (and ragtime's stepchild jazz) represented a "degeneration of music, having a 'disintegrating and demoralizing' effect," or was rather "constructive and progressive . . . a healthful music of the soil, having its rightful and beneficent place" (Farwell, 1912). The conclusion he reached — that the attempt to judge the moral or social impact of a music idiom tended to contaminated by social agendas — was a prescient analysis of arbiters' motives: "The question becomes one entirely of standpoint . . . Certainly no standpoint for such judgement can be tenable which bases itself upon self or class interest" (Farwell, 1912). Yet, as had been done with choral music, band music, and the solo piano repertoire, critics attempted to use moral functionalism driven by classist perspectives to assess jazz's impact. In so doing, they reified a rationale for using music in the service of shaping young people's tastes, conflating "taste" with "morality."[30] Eventually, supporters and opponents alike accepted the potential of these genres as educational tools, and argued their adaptability to good ends or ill.[31] Detractors linked the metaphorically unprofitable with the morally reprehensible,[32] and the "debit / credit" metaphor cited above with a metaphor of music as a tool for shaping morality.[33] Such linguistic moralism facilitated rather Puritanical evaluative conclusions: "Certain it is that which ["our Western culture"] prizes most highly, and that not alone in its arts, has been made possible at the price of renunciation of the more immediately appealing" (Laubenstein 1929). For such critics, aesthetic renunciation was mandatory to make moral quality possible; conversely, aesthetic accessibility "proved" unsuitability.

Assimilation of these music genres into the American academy required excision and replacement of semiotic associations; such reinterpretation was accomplished by imposition of evaluative criteria alien and inappropriate to the original vernacular contexts. The Romantic individualism of the solo piano repertoire, the bourgeois and functional associations of band music, the functionality of choral music, the sensuality and ethnicity of jazz, have all provoked semiotic strategies and critical language which invoked and manipulated class,[34] race,[35] or gender.[36] As Horowitz put it in 1975, "The symbols of the argument are etymological (terminological), yet the substance . . . is profoundly connected with racial (also classist and sexist) struggles in twentieth century America."

Ultimately this debate is central to understanding 20th-century American academic history because it is a debate about power and identity. It is about who wields the power to define American cultural identity, to articulate and evaluate cultural aspirations, to assign and withhold cultural value. The university has been a crucial symbolic arena in the construction of our semiotic landscape; academic institutions have held powerful control over evaluative status, and over the fiscal, political, and demographic privileges such status confers. Vernacular idioms co-opted by academia gained status but lost context, function, and social impact; they became another canonic collection in the museum of cultural objects, far from the fields of interplay and communication in which they originated. Understanding the motives, process and history of this semiotic colonialism seems an important initial step toward its redress.

References

Asmus, Edward P., Jr. 1980. "The Origin of the School Band Movement – Test". *The Instrumentalist* 34/6): 29, 31–32, 34.

Bain, Wilfred C. 1938. *The Status and Function of a cappella Choirs in Colleges and Universities in the United States.* Ed. D diss., New York University.

Borowicz, Jon T. 1990. "The Mid-Nineteenth Century Brass Band — A Rebirth". *Historic Brass Society Journal* 2: 123–31.

Boyd, Earl W. 1952. "Administrative Policies for the College and University Band". *Journal of Research in Music Education* 1–2: 56–58.

Citron, Marcia. 1993. *Gender and the Musical Canon.* Cambridge: Cambridge University Press.

Dean, Winton. 1990. *Handel's Dramatic Oratorios and Masques.* Oxford: Oxford University Press.

Farwell, Arthur. 1912. The Ethics of "Ragtime." *Musical America* 16/7: 24.

Gale, Harlow. 1922. "Musical Education". *Musical Quarterly* 8/1: 96–107.

Grainger, Percy. 1924. "What Effect is Jazz Likely To Have Upon the Music of the Future?", *The Etude Music Magazine* 42: 593–94.

Harding, Austin A. 1915. "The Band as a Community Asset". *Music Teachers National Association Volume of Proceedings.* Hartford, Conn., 189–90.

Horowitz, Irving L., and Charles Nanry. 1975. "Ideologies and Theories About American Jazz". *Journal of Jazz Studies* 2/2: 24–41.

"Jazz and Ragtime are the Preludes to a Great American Music". 1920. *Current Opinion* 69: 199–201.

Kapfer, Miriam B. 1968. "Elementary School Bands in Columbus, Ohio, and the Columbian Celebration of 1892". *Journal of Band Research* 5: 4–7.

Lang, Paul Henry. 1949. *Musical Quarterly* 35/4: 602–608.

Laubenstein, Paul F. 1929. "Jazz: Debit and Credit". *Musical Quarterly* 15: 606–24.

Loesser, Arthur. 1954. *Men, Women, and Pianos.* New York.

Lott, R. Allen. 1986. "The American Concert Tours of Leopold de Meyer, Henri Herz, and Sigismond Thalberg". Ph.D. diss., City University of New York.

MacIntyre, Alasdair. 1981. *After Virtue.* Notre Dame and Indianapolis: University of Notre Dame Press.

Mangrum, Mary G. 1969. "Experiences as a Violin Soloist with the Sousa Band". *The Instrumentalist* 24/3: 27–29.

Marquis, Arnold. 1971. "A Famous Civil War Band Lives Again". *The Instrumentalist* 25/11: 26–27.

McCarrell, Lamar K. 1972. "The Birth of U.S. College Bands". *The Instrumentalist* 27/3: 31–33.

McCarrell, Lamar K. 1973. "The Impact of World War II upon the College Band". *Journal of Band Research* 9: 3–8.

McCarrell, Lamar K. 1976. "Pioneer College Bands". *The Instrumentalist* 30/6: 34–35.

"Music's Place in America's Industrial Life". 1916. *Musical America* 24/7: 3–4.

Mussulman, Joseph A. 1979. *Dear People ... Robert Shaw: a Biography.* Bloomington: Indiana University Press.

Nevin, Gordon B. 1929. "Jazz — Wither Bound?" *The Etude Music Magazine* 47: 655 & 699.

Odom, Janice. 1972. "Twenty-Five Years of Respect for Jazz Education 1947–1972". *N.A.J.E. Jazz Educators Journal* 4/4: 9–10, 20 & 25.

Patterson, Frank. 1922. ""Jazz" — The National Anthem?" *Musical Courier* 84/18: 18; 84/19: 6.

Remarks on Rag-Time. 1913. *The Musical Courier* 66/22: 22–23.

Scott, Wayne. 1964. "The Stage Band in College". *The Instrumentalist* 18: 74–75.

Stringham, Edwin J. 1926. Jazz: "An Educational Problem". *Musical Quarterly* 12: 190–95.

Wagner, Lavern John. 1989. "The Humboldt, Kansas, Town Band: Its Times and its Music From 1866 to 1881". *Journal of Band Research* 23–24: 1–9.

Weber, Calvin E. 1967. "Albert Austin Harding: Pioneer College Bandmaster". *Journal of Band Research* 4: 5–12.

Wheaton, Jack. 1970. "Jazz in Higher Education". *N.A.J.E. Jazz Educators Journal* 2: 9–10 & 28.

"Where is Jazz Leading America? Opinions of Famous Men and Women in and out of Music". 1924. *The Etude Music Magazine* 42: 517–18, 520 & 595–96.

Whiteman, Paul. 1924. "What is Jazz Doing to American Music?" *The Etude Music Magazine* 42: 523–24.

"Will Ragtime Save the Soul of the Native American Composer?" 1917. *Current Opinion* 59: 406–07.

Notes

1. Control of musical terminology and analytical methods are a crucial means of recon-textualization. Acquiring such power increases the cultural arbiter's ability to define an object or behavior's contextual meaning, and hence its hierarchical status. Therefore such "quantitative objectivity" is a powerful strategic weapon, because it takes arts phenomena out of the realm of personal subjectivity, and into one in which quantitative markers of value may be assigned, erased, added, subtracted, and totalled. Critics have, for example, compared the number of upper-structure tones in an idiom's harmonic vocabulary, and used the argument "more is better" to "prove" the genre's "greater value." Conversely, high sales figures for individual pieces of sheet music have been used to "prove" the relevance or greater value of a genre.

2. Certain repertoires were judged safe for acquisition, because as objects they were more limited, symbolically passive, quantifiable, and receptive to manipulation. In contrast, contemporaneous performers and compositions, because they operated without the aura of historical distance, were symbolically unstable. Moreover, it was impossible for the academic arbiter to cite prior third-party "eminent authorities" in support of specific evaluations of contemporary works.

3. See Dean (1990), chapter 7 ("The Oratorio and English Taste"), for an examination of this class/audience phenomenon: "This was the rising middle class, the world of commerce and the professions and all those . . . on whom the country's increasing prosperity conferred for the first time a certain independence. To this audience Handel addressed all the later oratorios."

4. The institutionalization of Handel as an English cultural icon generations before his music sought entrance into American academia made the Handelian oratorio the best possible candidate.

5. "[Palestrina] brought to the art the finishing touches, the technical completeness and above all the high spiritual expression that had been hitherto almost entirely neglected. While other composers had been struggling with the art form in a technical manner, it was left to Palestrina the task of bringing life blood and spirit to the art" (Bain 1938).

6. Shaw's definition of the choral art and the committed chorister are clear in the numerous "letters" he wrote his singers: " . . . You don't *join* the Collegiate Chorale. You *believe* it. It's very damn near a religion. It's a way of life. Either you feel the fellow next to you is an important human being, and you like him, and you try desperately to understand how he feels about what he sings about, and pool your creative passions to make something a damned sight bigger than either of you could make alone — or this isn't your kind of choir. Either the music you sing is torn out of you — or you ought not to be singing" (8 February 1943; quoted in Mussulman 1979).

7. The generations-old tradition of college choirs touring Europe provides more than an opportunity for student travel at little expense; it provides a validation of their musical efforts by the audiences presumed able to judge their quality — a judgment sought out by performing their audiences' music in their own churches and auditoriums.

8. Elitist prejudices come into play here: the vernacular, beer-drinking communality of the village band was regarded as inferior to the aestheticist, oligarchic communality of the idealized college experience. The social and experiential aspects which had given village band music its functional meaning and value in the lives of participants were exactly those targetted for excision.

9. "Especially do they merit the support of those who are interested in the *community music problem*" (Harding 1915; emphasis added).

10. Most music teachers had some experience with the 18th-century singing schools of William Billings et al. This factor, and the limited availability of instruments, meant that primary emphasis was placed on methods and techniques for choral singing (see Asmus 1980).

11. In addition to massive social, economic, political, and demographic shifts, the War had also introduced large numbers of adult males to training and rehearsal in hand instruments, performance practice, and music-writing.

12. The earliest band specifically associated with primary education had been formed in 1857 at the Farm and Trades School on Thompson's Island in Boston Harbor. Reflecting the pre-War inaccessibility of brass instruments, it consisted of "tissue-covered combs, three violins, and a Bass viol" (Historian 1950). It is significant that this band was founded at a vocational school not one aimed at general, professional, or advanced education.

13. Harding manipulated semiotic and cultural associations in order to legitimize band music in academia; John Philip Sousa developed his own strategy to sanitize band music as a respectable concert repertoire. They followed similar strategies of "legitimization by association" in the areas of repertoire — Harding transcribing opera excerpts and works of Richard Strauss, Sousa orchestral music of Wieniawski and Mendelssohn — and the semiotics of instruments: Harding, an architect of the modern concert band, added woodwinds, orchestral percussion and strings. In addition, Sousa employed a long roster of violin soloists whose youth, instrument, female gender, and public presentation were all calculated to argue the impeccable chastity of his music-making:

    When [Sousa] came to escort [the violin soloist] on the stage . . . he always took you [!!] in very courtly fashion and made some remark to make you smile, like: "Here comes the fairest of her sex!" (Mangrum 1969)

14. "Accordingly, the music of a drum and bugle corps should appeal to a lower stratum of musical taste that does band music" (Whitehill, 1969).

15. The Dean of one well-known Music School, asked to serve as presenter for a television program highlighting the enormously popular drums corps competition held in his University's stadium, chose to assert the genre's legitimacy by comparing it to opera. Had he truly believed that drum corps was a legitimate genre, no such assertion would have been necessary; had he known academic history, he might have refrained from evoking opera, an idiom whose own vernacular, socially-functional, and mercantile origins have themselves been transubstantiated.

16. The influence of gender on musical thinking is as important in this period as in any other. The list of essential research on this relationship is too long to cite here, but one might begin with Citron (1993).

17. Lott (1986) concludes that mid-century American audiences received touring piano virtuosos and their repertory in much the same way as European audiences received Franz Liszt and others.

18. While male music students were present in academia, the study of "classical" music was, and still is, perceived as an activity more appropriate to women than to men.

19. "Great works" at this point becomes synonymous with "great man" since great men write great works and great works can only be written by great men. Note the parallels to Albert Austin Harding's invocation of the "great man" aesthetic in band music.

20. Bebop, and more recently New Orleans jazz, are seen as great repertories; Duke Ellington, Charlie Parker, and 1960s-era Miles Davis can be taken as examples of great practitioners or composers. For an example of canonizing impulses, consider the phenomena of repertory bands, and the advent of the "Young Lions": these are young, technically facile players whose musical approaches are sometimes criticized for excessive or imitative homage to great predecessors.

21. "This form of music . . . has been denounced far and wide as being of immoral character and having within it the means of inducing immorality. Nothing is so absurd. Music itself . . . has no inherent moral basis; it is a matter of use and association" (Stringham 1926).

22. It should be noted that the received historical view of ragtime's original reception in the popular press is drastically oversimplified. The usual formulation is that, in this new idiom, black and white ragtime composers expressed an effective aspiration to greater compositional sophistication, and that the validity of this attempt was ignored by race-and class-conscious cultural spokespersons (critics, white academic musicians, etc). In fact, the advent of ragtime precipitated a spirited, insightful, and by no means one-sided public debate on the idiom's origins, functions, and meaning. There is extensive primary material which suggests that many cultural arbiters showed sophisticated and sympathetic insight into the music's origins, innovations, and potential value as part of the American musical landscape; see, for instance, Farwell (1912), Engel (1922), Laubenstein (1929) and the contributions by Beach, Borowski, Cadman, Carpenter, Finck, Grainger, and Sousa in the 1924 special issue of *Etude* discussed immediately below. A close examination and subsequent reappraisal of the original public debate over ragtime is long overdue.

23. Rhythm was assessed the lowest, "common" denominator, the least valued component of a genre's presumed inherent value. Hence, jazz, a music which displayed decided rhythmic sophistication, gained no legitimacy thereby. Melody is placed in the evaluative middle of the technical hierarchy, but is described as farthest-ranging in terms of quality. That is, melody can be good, conforming adequately to Eurocentric evaluative criteria, or very bad, conforming inadequately to such criteria. Because jazz melody did not conform to European models, it accrued no quality thereby. Harmony is ranked highest in the pantheon of qualitative criteria, yet despite recognition by other critics of jazz's harmonic sophistication, the *Etude* discounts its contrasted harmonic language as inferior.

24. "The experimental spirit which has meant so much for national progress, particularly along scientific lines, in jazz receives encouragement" (Laubenstein 1929).

25. "The future of jazz may to a considerable degree be bound up with its frankly experimental mood . . . ([Though] there is a kind of deliberateness and self-consciousness, a disinterestedness in the concept 'experiment,' which has no part nor inheritance in either vital music or vital religion)" (Laubenstein 1929).

26. "These musicians prefer to regard themselves as beings apart. This is a pretty serious accusation for the musician to level against himself" (*Current Opinion* 1917).

27. "Why applaud the *Czardas* . . . or the dances from the Volga or the Danube, and at the same time seek to repudiate a growing musical art spring fresh and original from our native soil?" (Current Opinion, 1920)

28. Subsequent university focus on the big band repertoire, rather than chamber jazz of various types, permitted former travelling professionals to exercise and teach the same skills they had used in the 1930s and 40s on bandstands across the country. Moreover, the big band idiom was well-suited to a range of technical facilities, post-War band instruments were widely and cheaply available, charts could be written at various skill levels, and a band program was economical, necessitating only one faculty director/conductor per 14–22 players.

29. " . . . using the word [ragtime] in its generic sense as implying the whole field of cheap popular music" (Farwell 1912).

30. "The boys and girls of today are the men and women of tomorrow; and as taste, culture and refinement become part of the daily life in mature years, the appeal to good tastes cannot be applied too soon" (Woods 1924).

31. "So we see how association plays a large part in determining the moral character of music, and it cannot be proved that jazz . . . is immoral. It may be put to immoral use; but that is aside from the inherent capabilities of the mere musical notes . . . Jazz is in need of guidance into true, wholesome channels wherein it may be developed into what we would like to have it" (Stringham, 1926).

32. "The young pupil who attempts to play much of the 'raw' jazz of the day wastes time with common, cheap, trite tunes badly arranged. The pupil plays carelessly and 'sloppily'. These traits, once rooted, are very difficult to pull out. This is the chief evil of Jazz in music education" (*Etude* 1924).

33. "What frequently happens is that the greater gravity of the lower and easier standards pulls down the higher ones, or new standards of a relatively lower order are evolved and conformed to" (Laubenstein 1929).

34. "The fundamental idea seems to be that if you can pervert the taste of ten million persons in these United States — no matter how inferior they are as a class — into liking a thing, you may then, with the fervor of a religious zealot, call the thing American" (J. C. Bowman letter rebutting Moderwell, *Current Opinion* 1917).

35. The following quotation exhibits a particularly virulent example of the racist and ethnocentric values which attached to this discussion: "Jazz is to real music what the caricature is to the portrait. . . . When jazz was adopted by the 'highly civilized' white race, it tended to degenerate it towards primitivity. When a savage distorts his features and paints his face . . . we smile at his childishness; but when a civilized man imitates him, not as a joke but in all seriousness, we turn away in disgust" (Frank Damrosch; *Etude* 1924).

36. Some of the complex semiotics involved are revealed in a hoary jazz metaphor: 1) In 1925 the Whiteman/Gershwin "Rhapsody in Blue" collaboration was claimed by Whiteman himself to have "finally made a lady out of jazz" (Whiteman 1924); 2) 45 years later (1970), at ceremonies marking the foundation of the National Association of Jazz Educators, Merideth Wilson said jazz had "made a lady of a gal with a rather shady past" (Wheaton 1970); 3) In 1972, referring to the seminal role of the model jazz education program at North Texas State University, trumpeter, jazz educator, and former Ellington sideman Clark Terry claimed: "NTSU is the one school that really struck its neck out and made a respectable lady out of jazz" (Odom 1972). A peculiar and complex network of semiotic associations are embedded in the above metaphor, which has demonstrated remarkable longevity over most of the genre's history:

If jazz was presumed to require legitimization in order to become a "lady," then the genre must formerly have been presumed "less than" a lady; that is, of loose or free values — by default, a prostitute, who in the academic perspective had no perceived purpose other than as a sexual appliance. Jazz is thus portrayed as a purely functional genre with without immanent value. To become a "good woman," the genre of jazz was required a) to be purified of its former commercial/vernacular/functional meanings, and b) to elicit the mentorship of "good men" who would redeem "Her" from Her shameful former incarnation. However, such a reincarnative process denies both a person's, or a genre's, internal value. She becomes a fantasy of passivity, to be used as sexual appliance or remade as domestic trophy. Thus the advocates of jazz's academic legitimization were Pygmalions of gender, fantasizing the rescue of a "fallen woman" from her shameful original environments, behaviors, and motivations, and reincarnation in a pure, pacified, obedient new persona.

Contemporary Music Review
2000, Vol. 19, Part 1, pp. 113–140
Reprints available directly from the publisher
Photocopying permitted by license only

Re-Drawing Boundaries:
The Kronos Quartet

Dave Headlam

This article explores the phenomenon of the Kronos Quartet, principally through their recordings, and discusses how, in adopting some features of popular music while retaining elements of their classical heritage, they have redefined conventional musical and cultural notions of the string quartet. This study also argues that Kronos has helped to establish a hybrid, cross-cultural style that might be called "world minimalism" — a style that combines musical traits shared among some world musics with analogous elements found in classical minimalism. The critical literature on the group is considered, especially the charge that the quartet exhibits "postmodern sterility"; although certain pieces in their repertoire might be described as "postmodern," and while they have been described as a postmodern group in the mass media, the Kronos quartet is actually thoroughly modernist in its approach and presentation, drawing strongly on its classical heritage. The article concludes by arguing that the long-term effect of the Kronos Quartet's existence has been a substantial re-drawing of the boundaries that existed in recorded music, and that their belief in and promotion of contemporary music has been an extremely beneficial force in the music world.

KEYWORDS: Kronos Quartet, string quartet, crossover, world music, twentieth-century music, minimalism

Despite a few appearances in the sphere of popular music — in the Beatles' song "Yesterday" for instance — the string quartet has until relatively recently been the quintessential exemplar of the "classical" music ideal of music for musicians, subject to refined, concentrated listening in contemplative settings removed from the distractions of society. Thus, it is remarkable that the genre has not only been reinvigorated, but has become a symbol of a new direction in "art" music, wherein art and popular music — the latter expanded to include so-called "world music" — have become intertwined to a degree unprecedented in this century. This new role for the string quartet is due largely to the musical and marketing influence of the Kronos Quartet, now over two decades old. From its concerts and recordings, commissions and collaborations, repertoire including such diverse composers as Alfred Schnittke, John Zorn, Anton Webern, and Jimi Hendrix, and contemporary post-punk image and theatrical stage presentation, Kronos has gained a popularity and influence substantial enough to redefine the terms of classical-music recordings and concerts. In its ability to "cross over" from the classical charts to a wider audience, Kronos follows in the wake of John Cage and Leonard Bernstein, minimalist composers such as Steve Reich, Philip Glass, and John Adams, and a larger trend towards a mixing of musical categories that includes such groups as the Who (with their rock "opera" *Tommy*), Tashi, and the Turtle Island Quartet (one of many string quartets which has appeared in Kronos' wake), and figures as diverse as Laurie Anderson, Elvis Costello, Danny Elfman, Nigel Kennedy, Michael Nyman, Luciano Pavoratti, Frank Zappa, Keith Emerson, and John Zorn. In its impact on its own genre and increasing tendency to transform and transcend that genre, Kronos has even been compared to the Beatles (Tesser 1987, 16).

The success of the Kronos quartet in concert and recordings has helped to redefine the boundaries between the classical and popular-music worlds — at the same time that the boundaries of both are being reset to include world music.[1] It has in fact become ever more problematic to distinguish between art and popular music, and the appellation "world" music, generally applied to musical elements not from the Western European tradition, has proved woefully inadequate. A visit to a local recorded music venue bears out this assertion: the previously simple divisions into rock, jazz, country, and classical have been replaced by a bewildering array of styles and hybrids, and Gregorian chant appears beside a Led Zeppelin box set while *Nirvana Unplugged* is highlighted along with a re-release of standards by recent Grammy-winner Tony Bennett, a CD of Brazilian music produced by David Byrne, and a collection of Eastern Asian *Night Prayers* by the Kronos Quartet.

In this article, I will explore the phenomenon of the Kronos quartet, principally through their recordings, discussing first how, in adopting some features of popular music while retaining elements of their classical heritage, they have redefined conventional musical and cultural notions of the string quartet. Their explorations of music ranging from Philip Glass to Arvo Pärt and Terry Riley to Bill Evans have achieved an unprecedented level of popularity with both college crowds and baby boomers, and opened the door for the largely conservative classical chamber music world to expand. Second, I hope to demonstrate how Kronos has helped to establish a hybrid, cross-cultural style that might be called "world minimalism" — a style that combines musical traits shared among some world musics with analogous elements found in classical minimialism. Third, I will engage the critical literature on the group, responding to the charge of a postmodern sterility by noting that although certain pieces in their repertoire might be described as "postmodern," and while they have been described as a postmodern group in the mass media, the Kronos quartet is actually thoroughly modernist in its approach and presentation, drawing more strongly on their classical heritage in this context. Finally, I conclude that the long-term effect of the Kronos Quartet's existence has been a substantial re-drawing of the boundaries that existed in recorded music, and that their belief in and promotion of contemporary music has been an extremely beneficial force in the music world.

Introduction

The Kronos Quartet — the name is from the Greek god of time, Chronos — was formed in 1973 in Seattle by violinist David Harrington. The quartet resided at the State University of New York at Geneseo (near Rochester) from 1975, moving to San Francisco in 1977and adding a new cellist and second violinist to arrive at the current personnel of Harrington and John Sherba, violins, Hank Dutt, viola, and Joan Jeanrenaud, cello.[2] The group has since held residencies at Mills College (1978–80) and the Arnold Schoenberg Institute at the University of Southern California, where they played concerts, worked with composition faculty and students, and coached quartets; they continue to visit colleges and universities, combining performances with master classes. In the mid-1980s, Kronos produced a series of thirty-six hour-long radio programs for American Public Radio, featuring performances and rehearsals, interviews and conversations, and, as Harringon (1995) has noted, the opportunity to combine diverse musics in varying proportions as a training ground for their later recordings.

The quartet is self-managed by the Kronos Performing Arts Association, a non-profit foundation dedicated to contemporary music and performance. Taking it upon themselves to discover new ways of performing contemporary music, Kronos members commission new works, often as part of extended collaborations in rehearsal with composers, and choose from among many unsolicited manuscripts to perform new works with each concert series. Kronos has performed in such diverse situations as playing the national anthem before a baseball game in San Francisco, presenting a season of concerts since 1982 at San Fransciso's Herbst Theatre, and even joining forces with Elvik, an eight-foot robot with a revolving head, to play some James Brown tunes (Tesser 1987, 16). For their encores, they have played "The Shower Scene" from the movie *Psycho*, a medley of 1950s pop tunes titled "Opus 50," and "Purple Haze" and "Foxy Lady" by Jimi Hendrix. They have been critically acclaimed, winning multiple awards for their recordings, including the New York Times and USA Today Awards of "Best of the Year," Grammaphon Critic's Choice, and Grammy nominations and awards.

An appreciation for the change in attitude represented by the Kronos Quartet can be gained by leafing through the publications *Chamber Music* and *Strad*. In these pages, the traditional tuxedoes-and-long-dresses image of classical musicians and Germanic 18th- and 19th-century repertoire still dominates, alongside articles that simultaneously celebrate this heritage and warn of diminishing audiences and the need for innovation.[3] In interviews, members of Kronos have addressed this issue, and how they consciously have worked to update the image of their genre. In response to a question about the initial impulse behind the Kronos quartet, violinist David Harrington noted the conventional images that he strove to change:

[In my early experiences] it was pretty clear that the world of quartets was pretty much dying. . . . I remember in high school, where I first started a quartet when I was 12, . . . and I remember when I used to go to some of the concerts, . . . it was so bizarre to be the youngest person there, to be hearing all this fantastic music and just have this idea that it was not part of the time or our culture. I think it was a real appendage, a distant appendage at that; that always seemed strange to me . . . still does. It just seemed like it was something that only old people liked. I never liked the way that quartets were portrayed in the media; it was generally these old guys who looked like they were tired out and overweight, like those New Yorker cartoons kind of bullshit — I hated it, I hated it. I still do; that's not what this music is about . . . it's not the Sunday-afternoon, white-gloved-crowd approach." (Harrington 1995)

In the image they project to their audience, the Kronos quartet has taken an obvious yet radical approach. In the typical classical venue, where the piece and composer are the points of focus, the dress, formal atmosphere, behavioral code, and relationship of performing ensemble and audience and are usually set and followed rigidly (Shumway 1992, 122). Rather than re-creating the typically exaggerated American version of an idealized "European" concert setting with its hushed, historic atmosphere, as is the custom among the devotees of the classical music world, the Kronos quartet members dress in contemporary style, looking as if they actually live in the 1990s rather than the 1820s, with stage lighting and setting that emphasize a hip and casual atmosphere. The favorable audience response to this approach has sent many classical music labels back to the advertising drawing board (Stark 1991).[4]

The group's success has derived not only from presenting the string quartet in a new light, but from making their concerts both participatory

and challenging events — two characteristics that are mutually rein-
forcing, but in which the latter must follow from the former. The participatory strategy derives most immediately from the aesthetics of rock
music, where the audience's initial individual response to Kronos's
presentation of themselves, their music, and their stage setting as contemporary evolves into a communal sense of identity and empower-
ment from the bonding of individual audience members sharing the
experience into a group. When the Kronos quartet played at the Eastman
School of Music a few years ago, for instance, the musicians entered in a
theatrical setting that audience members could clearly identify with as
hip and happening, creating a sense of excitement and group focus that
was striking compared to the usual objective and somewhat detached
atmosphere found at the countless numbers of "classical" recitals that
take place. The response was closer to rock festivals, opera, or theater,
where audiences enter a make-believe world and participate in it fully
(Shumway 1992, 123).[5]

This level of identification on the part of college- and middle-aged
audiences, both of whom associate the charged atmosphere with their
own experiences of popular music, is an important element in the group's
continued success. However, as Madonna, Peter Gabriel, David Byrne,
and Paul Simon from the popular music world have clearly demonstrated, contemporary audiences demand constant change and challenge as
well. Their embrace of such diversity and challenge is the second important aspect of the Kronos phenomenon. From the begininng, members
have noted the intentional programming of new and difficult pieces in a
continual stream. This type of programming flies in the face of the supposedly safe route of continually replaying "classics" adopted by many
larger classical music organizations. According to violist Hank Dutt,
"People come to our concerts expecting to be challenged" (Jepson 1986,
88). Harrington agrees: "When people come to a Kronos concert they
know they will hear something that requires a reaction, even if they don't
like that they are hearing. You can't just sit back and relax" (Elson 1989,
86). "Our concerts will not be comforting but exploratory, something that
people will not have any prior experience of. I want to change their ideas
about what our music means; about what any music means" (Pendergast
1992, 43).

The music Kronos presents is not only challenging, but eclectic. Their
concerts and a number of their releases consist of varied compilations in
which the only unifying thread is the group itself. This focus on the performers rather than the music differs from many classical music recordings, which, even with established performers, often tend to be organized
around a famous composer, genre, or time period.[6] In this focus on the
performers and the presentation, Kronos borrows from the aesthetics of

popular music, particularly rock, where, as David R. Shumway (1992, 129) has noted, the performers are the "text, perhaps even the primary texts of the form," not just as musicians, but as part of all-encompassing "collaborative productions" (including staging, repertoire, promotion, etc.) that make up the medium. The focus on the "production" has been used in critical commentary on Kronos, even when their musicianship and committment is noted, as if they have somehow betrayed an essential aspect of classical music. Actually, they have merely adopted a successful tactic from popular music.

Another aspect of the Kronos quartet is their use of technology to explore new sounds and timbres. The striving for new timbres has in the past marked a notable difference between classical music, which has tended to be pitch and rhythm-based, and popular music — particularly rock — which has tended to be timbre and rhythm-based. The conventional string quartet has a uniform range of timbres within each instrument, but with a variety of sounds available by bowing and fingering effects. The latter were explored in music from the early 20th century, but in the 1950s and 1960s the possibilities for string sounds in combination were greatly expanded in pieces like Penderecki's "Threnody for the Victims of Hiroshima" and Steve Reich's "Violin Phase"; in 1970 another step forward was taken with George Crumb's "Black Angels," which calls for amplified instruments and innovative playing techniques (including recreating the sound of a consort of viols by holding the instruments vertically and bowing above the fingering hand). On the Kronos recording of "Black Angels," these sound possibilities are exploited in full in one of the group's most dynamic performances. On their release *Short Stories*, the piece "Digital" transforms the group into a typewriter, and a similar effect, but setting the quartet against the recorded sound of balls bouncing off strings, appears in Sofia Gubaidulina's Quartet no. 4 on the CD *Night Prayers*. In these and other pieces, the range of timbres demonstrates the group's active interest in the history and future of their instruments.

On "Spectre" (from the CD *Short Stories*), Kronos recorded raw material for the composer John Oswald, who manipulated it digitally in combination, creating "aggregations" of different forms of tone production to be played along with the group on the recording and in concert. The inclusion of this piece points to an important aspect of Kronos's use of technology. In conversation, Harrington has noted the willingness of Kronos to use altered sounds, but commented that their use is very much a musical decision: "it depends what we're looking for and what's in the music...its a way of taking the listener somewhere" (Harrington 1995).[7] Elsewhere, he has reiterated his strong feelings for the basic string quartet sound: "People are turning to this medium [string quartet] because of the palette of colors that has been developed and world of references that can be made. For me the string quartet sound is the most personal sound there is" (Young 1991, 999). In general, the sounds of the string instruments on Kronos recordings are altered less by electronics than by changes in context and surroundings, as the group adapts itself to different types of music — African, East Asian, Indian, etc. Thus, Kronos is largely able to perform the works on its recordings live on stage, augmenting the basic quartet with additional musicians where practical.[8] In this aspect, paraphrasing Robert B. Ray, the group adheres to the modernist approach to the live performance aesthetic of jazz and classical music rather than the recreation of a recording characteristic of much rock music, where the recording and even video come first and the performance is an attempt to replicate these set forms (Ray 1992, 145–46).[9]

The Music

A listing of Kronos-only recordings, including full-length compact discs (CDs) and shorter-length CD "singles" of the type commonly found in popular music, is given in Figure 1.[10] Their output can be divided into their appearances on single tracks in numerous releases (not given in Figure 1), their early releases on the Landmark and Grammavision labels, and their recordings on Elektra/Nonesuch records.[11] Their own recordings — those in which Kronos is either the only group or the focal group performing — can be categorized into collections, themes, single composers/pieces, and, somewhat more loosely, styles. Collections are here defined as groups of diverse pieces presented (as stated in the liner notes to *Kronos Quartet*, the initial release on Elektra Nonesuch) in the manner of an actual Kronos concert. This type of "studio-live" release is a somewhat unique concept. The "themes" and "styles" categories are also collections, but themes have an extramusical program connecting the pieces, as in the theme of war and struggle unifying "Black Angels", and styles are associated by musical or national characteristics, as in *Pieces of Africa* and the largely East Asian composers on *Night Prayers*. The greatest number of releases is dedicated to single composers or pieces: the minimalists Terry Riley and Steve Reich, South African native and African music-inspired Kevin Volans, Poles Witold Lutoslawski and Henryk Górecki, Bob Ostertag, and proto-minimalist Morton Feldman. Several of these releases also have social or political themes: the piece "All the Rage" by Bob Ostertag is dedicated to Gay and Lesbian Rights in the age of AIDS, and "Different Trains" by Steve Reich concerns the Holocaust.

Collections:

Kronos Quartet: In Formation (1979, 1982, 1990)	[KQ:IF] Reference RR-9CD	
Kronos Quartet (1986)	[KQ]	Elektra 79111
White Man Sleeps (1987)	[WMS]	Elektra 79169
Winter was Hard (1988)	[WwH]	Elektra 79181
Short Stories (1993)	[SS]	Elektra 79310
At the Grave of Richard Wagner (1993)	[GRW]	Elektra 79318

Themes:

Black Angels (1990) — war, suffering	[BA]	Elektra 79242

Single composer/piece:

Thelonius Monk: Monk Suite (1985)	[TM:MS]	Landmark 81505
Bill Evans, Music of Bill Evans (1986)	[BE]	Landmark 15102
Terry Riley, Cadenza on the Night Plain (1988)	[TR:CNP]	Gramavision 79444
Terry Riley, Salome Dances for Peace (1989)	[TR:SDP]	Elektra 79217
Steve Reich, Different Trains (1989)	[SR:DT]	Elektra 79176
Kevin Volans, Hunting, Gathering (1991)	[KV:HG]	Elektra 79253
Witold Lutoslawski, String Quartet (1991)	[WT:SQ]	Elektra 79255
Henryk Górecki (1993)	[HG]	Elektra 79319
Bob Ostertag, All the Rage (1993)	[BO:AR]	Elektra 79332
Morton Feldman, Piano and String Quartet (1993)	[MF:PSQ]	Elektra 79320
Philip Glass, Kronos Performs Philip Glass (1995)	[PG]	Elektra 79356

Style:

Astor Piazzolla: Five Tango Sensations (1991)	[AP]	Elektra 79254
Pieces of Africa (1992)	[PA]	Elektra 79275
Night Prayers (1993)	[NP]	Elektra 79346

Figure 1   Kronos only Releases

Modern or Postmodern? and What About "Purple Haze"?

In the repertoire usually associated with string quartets, we are used to finding "masterworks" by acknowledged "great" composers to compare with interpretations on countless other recordings, as well as to respond to as constant reaffirmations of the cultural fruits of Western civilization. Although infrequently mentioned in the literature, the Kronos Quartet has its own collection of twentieth-century "masterworks" sprinkled throughout its recordings; significantly, however, none appear on their first major-label release, *Kronos Quartet*. In a bold move which largely defined the group's priorities and identity, Kronos postponed the inclusion of a "great" work until their second recording, *White Man Sleeps*, which contains the String Quartet no. 3 by Béla Bartók. Other such works follow on subsequent releases: Anton Webern, "Six Bagatelles, Opus 9" (*WwH*) and "Five Pieces, Opus 5" (*GRW*), Samuel Barber, "Adagio" (*WwH*), George Crumb, "Black Angels" (*BA*), Dmitri Shostakovich, "String Quartet no. 8" (*BA*), Witold Lutoslawski, "String Quartet" (*WL:SQ*), and Alban Berg, "String Quartet, Opus 3" (*GRW*).[12] This category also includes little-known works by famous names: "Scherzo: Holding Your Own" by Charles Ives (*WMS*), "At the Grave of Richard Wagner" by Franz Liszt (for string quartet, piano, and harp) — as part of the collection of the same name which includes pieces by Webern and Berg, and is the only exclusively "master-composer" release by Kronos — and the "Quartet Euphometric" by Henry Cowell (*SS*).

In assessing the recordings by Kronos, this "masterwork" category could be enlarged still further to cover works by more recently famous composers: two works by Henryk Górecki, the "String Quartet no. 1, Opus 62: Already It Is Dusk," and the "String Quartet no. 2 Opus 64: Quasi una Fantasia," and the piece "Piano and String Quartet" by Morton Feldman, each with their own dedicated releases; a version of "Fratres" by Arvo Pärt (*WwH*); a quartet by Conlon Nancarrow (*Kronos Quartet*); the "String Quartet no. 3" by Alfred Schnittke (*WwH*); and two quartets by Sofia Gubaidulina, "Quartet no. 2" (*SS*) and "Quartet no. 4" (*Night Prayers*). Finally, pieces by the composers associated with the classical "minimalist" school, Terry Riley, Philip Glass, and Steve Reich may be added to this list. Viewed in this respect, as searching out and recording "great" new works, Kronos follows in the wake of the Kolisch, LaSalle, and Juilliard quartets.

In light of the sheer number of these "masterworks," it is worth considering the label "postmodern" that has been applied to the Kronos Quartet.[13] The label has been used in a critical context by Edward Rothstein, who in a commentary entitled "The Zeitgeist Quartet" comments that Kronos has even pursued the postmodernist attitude to its visuals, replacing the dour, staid vision of traditional string quartet members with equally dour expressions, but filtered through a rock-inspired sensibility to create "haunted visages" reflecting the "grim sorrows of our time" (Rothstein 1987).[14] In his view, much of their music — as with Kevin Volans's "White Man Sleeps," for instance — derives its effect not from the "nervous and inconsequential music" but from the title and political association — in this case, the composer's South African birthplace. Rothstein places Kronos in the chamber music lineage of Tashi, but whereas the earlier group was "guided by the structure of the music," and proceeded with "clear, unrelenting, logic," Kronos is adrift in a postmodern world in which all artistic products are commodities of equal value. The music, like folk music, presents a communal experience — akin to a rock concert — rather than a reflective or aesthetic one. The early repertoire, which includes examples from the folk-influenced composers Bartók, Shostakovich, and Ives, is typified by Ben Johnston's variations on "Amazing Grace" (*WMS*), where previous generations' folk music is put through the postmodern wringer. This postmodern world has no soul, however, Rothstein implies, and, like much popular music, reflects a bankrupt civilization.

Rothstein's criticism's, although hyperbolic, raise some interesting points. As noted, the Kronos quartet creates a communal concert experience akin to that quintessential latter 20th-century chamber music phenomenon, the rock group. This feature is undoubtedly at the root of their success with the baby-boomer generation, which has otherwise been stubbornly resistant to classical music (Royer 1989). Communal experiences, however, certainly do not preclude aesthetic or reflective ones. As for Volans's music deriving its effect from a political subtext rather than purely musical values, such a judgement is highly individual, and may also be attributed to Kronos's adoption of certain popular-music characteristics, such as emphasizing message over musical complexity. But more interesting is the larger question of whether the "postmodernist" label is even applicable to the Kronos quartet.

Most of the works in Kronos recordings are thoroughly "modernist" in their self-referential and unified construction and their secure historical context.[15] Arguable exceptions are the Schnittke and Crumb works, which, with their programmatic use of quotation and allusion, feature the elements of external reference couched in commentary usually associated with musical postmodernism. But the Kronos Quartet approaches even these works in a straightforwardly and energetically modernist fashion, with no postmodernist ironic or otherwise critical subtext. The same can be said for the recorded performances of all of Kronos's pieces; from "Purple Haze" by Jimi Hendrix through "Digital" by Elliot Sharp; the recordings project an aura of sincerity and earnest, dedicated, expression. In fact, the only truly postmodern works in the Kronos repertoire might be those composed by John Zorn — "Forbidden Fruit (Variations for Voice, String Quartet, and Turntable)" (*WwH*) and "Cat O' Nine Tails" (*SS*) — who juxtaposes music, speech (in different languages), and noises (familiar and unfamiliar) from different eras and styles and using old and new technologies, with a clearly satiric intent.

If not the individual pieces, the collections themselves might be given the label "postmodern." The initial release on the Elektra/Nonesuch label, *Kronos Quartet*, has been the impetus for this categorization: it includes works by Peter Schulthorpe and Aulis Sallinen which, as described below, combine minimalist and world music influences, an abstract minimalist quartet subtitled "Company" by Philip Glass, a traditionally modernist quartet by Conlon Nancarrow, and, most famously, an arrangement of "Purple Haze" by Jimi Hendrix. The features that have elicited the most commentary are the eclectic combination, lack of any "masterpieces," and the inclusion of the Hendrix arrangement. The former two features, as mentioned above, go against traditional marketing practices in classical music, where a new group is usually paired with a known repertoire or composer to attract the buying public, and only as a loyal following is built up is a more adventurous choice of works allowed. Thus, even the trendy and visually challenging English classical violinist Nigel Kennedy recorded the warhorse Vivaldi's *Four Seasons*, possibly the most recorded work in the repertoire, for his initial release. Kronos, however, based their eclectic release on their own concert reputation and attractiveness as a group. It was a risky strategy from a commercial standpoint, but one that has paid off.

Possibly the most notable feature on *Kronos Quartet* and undoubtedly the best-known recording by the group is "Purple Haze." Initial reviews are divided on this arrangement, which may have seemed like a gimmick to attract buyers until it became clear that the piece is part of Kronos's personality, and that it, as well as Hendrix's "Foxy Lady" and the "Opus 50" medley, had already been in the group's encore repertoire for years. "Purple Haze" (released by Hendrix in 1967) is music of the members' generation, and, in drawing Hendrix into the classical world, to the point of simulating guitar amplifier distortion with bowing effects, Kronos is the complement to progressive-rock groups like Emerson, Lake and Palmer and Yes in the 1970s. Following in the wake of albums like the Beatles' *Sgt. Pepper* (1967), which brought the string quartet, harpsichord, brass and other classical instruments — even the full orchestra — into the rock world within newly composed songs, these next-generation groups, with classically trained musicians Keith Emerson, Rick Wakeman, and others, recreated classical works, such as Bartók's "Allegro Barbaro," Brahms's Fourth Symphony (third movement), Copland's "Fanfare for the Common Man," Ginastera's Piano Concerto , Janáček's "Sinfonietta," and Mussorgsky's "Pictures at an Exhibition," in the timbres and rhythms of rock music. These crossover forays brought these groups the kind of pro and con critical commentary that has followed the Kronos quartet's similar move in the opposite musical direction.

In another view, however, the choice of "Purple Haze" is somewhat ironic. The world of rock music has developed and been institutionalized to the point that a canon of "masterworks" and "master composer/ performers" has been annointed, and even committed to a Hall of Fame (Gass 1992). Hendrix is often placed foremost among this exalted crowd, having even fulfilled the ultimate requirement of dying young, as a recognized "genius." Thus, in a sense, the Kronos quartet's first release contains only one true "classic" work — "Purple Haze." If the choice had been an inconsequential rock work, one unacknowledged by the establishment, then Edward Rothstein's critical attitude toward Kronos as a postmodern group would have had some validity. Rothstein's view is, however, incorrect. Kronos does not combine indiscriminately the droppings from various musical "movements"; rather, in their first and subsequent releases they take a modernist approach with a strong historical bias toward the present and toward a level of commitment to advancing the state of the art and to technical perfection that is distinctly at odds with postmodernism.

Even granting the discussion above, the choice of "Purple Haze" as a built-in encore on their first major release on a new label does, of course, show a boldness of vision and purpose, and a desire to create new conventions and break old boundaries. It is not, however, characteristic of the group's later recordings, which have tended toward new works written exclusively for Kronos.[16] The only other notable "cover" version found in the following Kronos recorded output is the arrangement by Steven Mackey of Willie Dixon's "Spoonful" (*SS*). The choice of this particular piece is, however, quite significant and characteristic of the group's output in larger terms. Dixon is an important figure in music history for a number of reasons. For one, he was a pivotal member of the Chicago electric blues scene of the late 1940s to early 1960s — a scene that heavily influenced the development of rock music both in Britain and the United States in the late 1950s and 1960s, inspiring such seminal figures as Chuck Berry and Eric Clapton, and groups such as the Rolling Stones, Yardbirds, Who, Cream, and Led Zeppelin (Dixon 1989).[17] Dixon was a prolific and acknowledged composer, performer, and producer in a setting in which authorship was not usually recognized, and many original performers, arrangers, or composers were routinely ripped off by producers and record companies.[18] The ongoing critical and monetary acknowledgment of the African American roots of rock music — and the authorship of musicians like Dixon — has been and continues to be an important development in the American popular-music world. By recording Dixon's song "Spoonful" (which has been "covered" by many groups) Kronos places itself within the unfolding of this history from the unique perspective of a classical group and refers back to the earlier cover release of "Purple Haze."

"World Minimalism" and Political Themes

In their popularity and choice and combination of composers and repertoire, the Kronos has helped to disseminate a hybrid style of music which might be described as "world minimalist."[19] The latter of these terms, minimalism, refers to a movement in music dating from the late 1950s, described by Edward Strickland as superceding "serialism" and "post-serialism" as the next "classic" period of music. Strickland describes minimalism as a music in which "severity of means, clarity of form, [and] simplicity of structure and texture" meet in a context "prone to stasis [and] resistant to development," tending to "decontextualization from tradition, impersonality in tone, and flattening of perspective" (Strickland 1993, 3–7). Although the modernist tone of this description reflects the fact that the central figures of minimalism emerged from the serialist 1950s, each of them was also influenced by popular and non-western musics: from the "godfathers" John Cage and Lou Harrison, who were interested in Eastern philosophies and music, to composers La Monte Young, Terry Riley, Steve Reich, and Philip Glass, who have acknowledged influences ranging through Japanese *Gagaku* music, Webern's aphoristic statements, Schoenberg's Orchestra Piece Opus 16/III with its *Klangfarbenmelodie* focus on sound and timbre, the modal jazz of Miles Davis and John Coltrane, tape and electronic music, and musics of India, North Africa, Bali, and Israel, particularly Ravi Shankar's sitar and tabla combinations, African drumming, Balinese Gamelan, and Hebrew Cantillation (Strickland 1993). Thus, from the beginning, minimalism has included elements of "world" music, and the minimalist and post-minimalist composers favored by Kronos have tended to pursue the social, political, and cultural aspects of world music while maintaining and fostering musical similarities between classical minimalism and these world elements.

"World" music has, of course, long been the purview of ethnomusicology, but the more recent association of musical elements from many countries with popular music, jazz and particularly rock, as in recent recordings by Peter Gabriel, David Byrne, and Paul Simon among others, has led to an unprecedented widespread interest and popularity. Scholarly studies have proliferated and established some useful distinctions and categories when discussing such music. In the collection, *World Music, Politics and Social Change*, editor Simon Frith has noted the distinction between music studied from within and from without its own cultural and linguistic context, and in the same volume Charles Hamm has focused on African music, describing the extent to which studies have taken their lead from performances of African music in the west, or recordings produced for export or by musicians who have left Africa. Both writers avoid judgments on these issues, and in fact emphasize the impossibility of ascertaining any "pure" or "traditional" status for music or of assuming simplistic models of evolution from folk music to art music or corruption from pure or traditional music to commodity or popular music (Frith 1989 and Hamm 1989).[20] Their comments form a background for any discussion of "world" music elements in recordings by the Kronos quartet. To an unavoidable extent, even on compilations such as *Pieces of Africa*, the musical works are subjected to a level of modernist objectification in their removal from cultural context and thus become aesthetic objects. It is in this sense that the musical elements of world music are here compared with those of minimalism.

On *Kronos Quartet* (1986), the combination of Peter Sculthorpe's world music-influenced String Quartet no. 8 and Philip Glass's abstract "classic" minimalist Quartet no. 2 "Company" establishes a link and sets the tone for many subsequent Kronos recordings. The musical materials in the five-movement quartet by Sculthorpe, upon which the composer publicly acknowledges the influence of Balinese music, may be diagramed as "AB(bab)A'BA(b)" (Sandow 1986). The "A"/"a" material, related to the Balinese *arja*, is a slow, intense, soloistic music either unaccompanied or accompanied by a drone bass with surrounding atmospheric gestures in altered sounds such as harmonics or pizzicato. The "B"/"b" material, related to the Balinese "ketungen" or "rice-pounding music," is a complex, pulsating, rhythmically active, *moto perpetuo* music employing the full ensemble in a thick texture, incorporating varied timbres from the string instruments. The dramatic contrast and alternation of these two textures is characteristic of many Kronos pieces. On their later release *Night Prayers*, for instance, the "Lacrymosa" (as described in the liner notes by composer Dmitri Yanov-Yanovsky) consists of dual "realities" in the quartet and soprano parts (performed by Dawn Upshaw): "the voice is free, unpredictable, like the song of the whale, while the quartet is in constant repetition, contained, bound by rules. What I wanted to do was... unite two different realities, to connect the unconnectable" (Yanov-Yanovsky 1994). The two forces of the soloistic voice and active quartet — similar to the alternating long melody and minimalist activity found in the Sculthorpe piece — begin separately but come together (4' 10") only to separate again (4' 29"). A similar contrast of a solo line, on cello, set against group activity is found in "Mugam Sayagi" by Franghiz Ali-Zadeh (*NP*), where the cello represents a woman's voice and the remainder of the group a surrounding community.

These two textures, found in many Kronos pieces, are also two central features of minimalism in its original formation. As described by Strickland, the textures of La Monte Young's early "String Trio," consist of long-tone expositions, with expanses of time containing few actual note changes; rather, extended note groups change exceedingly slowly (Strickland 1993). This texture is similar to the condensed, lyric writing of Morton Feldman, who wrote his *Piano and String Quartet* for the Kronos Quartet. The other texture is of active, rapid, rhythmic, repeating modules in a largely diatonic or modal context developed by Terry Riley and used most notably in his work *In C* (1964), which influenced the pulsing music of Steve Reich and Philip Glass.

Following the Sculthorpe work on *Kronos Quartet* (1986), the Glass piece clearly cements the relationship between world-influenced and minimalist musics and sets out one of the main sonic spaces that Kronos explores in subsequent recordings. Unlike the programmatic Sculthorpe piece, however, Glass's "Company" (String Quartet no. 2) lacks movement labels: all that is given are tempo designations, quarter = 96, then 160, 90, and 160 again. In this abstract work, the patterning is clearly audible, with the relatively simple rhythms and continual, consistent articulation characteristic of the pulsing type of minimalism. Kronos returned to Glass's string quartets in *Kronos Quartet Performs Philip Glass* (1995), re-recording "Company" (String Quartet no. 2), and adding "Mishima" (String Quartet no. 3, part of which had appeared in an earlier recording by Kronos of Glass's incidental music to *Mishima*), "Buczak" (String Quartet no. 4), and the String Quartet no. 5. The textural and gestural variety in the latter quartet indicates the extent of Glass's growth from the continual classical minimalist pulsing and arpeggios in his Quartet no. 2.

The companion modernist "minimal" abstract work to the Glass pieces in the Kronos recordings is Morton Feldman's "Piece for Piano and String Quartet." Feldman's spare texture consists of repeated arpeggios on the piano overlapping with sustained chords in the quartet; the impression moment to moment is that nothing changes, but over time the spatial and chronological relationship between the two forces is altered; at times the piano or the quartet sounds alone (at 35' 30" and 29' 10", respectively), at times the two sound together. The piece lasts 79' 33" with the slow unfolding over time familiar from classical minimalism. The Glass and Feldman works are the only "abstract" minimalist pieces recorded by Kronos; in general their minimalist tendencies are encased in world music or political or thematic exteriors, as in the Reich piece "Different Trains."

The world-music direction provided by the Sculthorpe piece is continued with the Volans "White Man Sleeps" (*WMS*). This piece, which recalls the faster, more active sections in the Sculthorpe quartet, returns in a completed version on *Pieces of Africa*, with Volans's music also featured on the CD single *Hunting: Gathering*. The trend toward world music culminates in the highly successful *Pieces of Africa*, with music by eight composer/performers, in which Kronos interweaves the string quartet with African instruments and vocals. Musically, the combinations present an intriguing meeting ground for the forces of minimalism and traditional song forms along with African rhythms and melodies. The almost ubiquitous presence of vocals reminds listeners of the intensely vocal associations of string instruments in folk cultures.

Strikingly different from the *Pieces of Africa* collection, where the themes are renewal, family, the bonds between people and the earth, ceremony, and celebration, are the songs on *Night Prayers*, where the composers stem largely from Central Asian countries formerly part of the Soviet Union. Here the themes are sadness, separation, and struggle, with oppressed peoples and cultures disappearing under threat of war, and with nature images now only reminders of a happier past or hoped-for future. (The exception is the Gubaidulina "Quartet no. 4," an abstract study that combines the quartet with prepared sounds, as described below.) In this aspect, *Night Prayers* recalls the themes of war and struggle in the earlier *Black Angels* collection, which includes: 1) the title piece by George Crumb written in response to the Vietnam war; 2) the 40-part motet "Spem in Alium" by Thomas Tallis with its theme of averted invasion (and a rare step outside the twentieth century for Kronos); 3) the moving "Doom. A Sigh" by Istvan Marta based around actual folk songs from a displaced peoples called Csangos (part of a community of Hungarians in the village of Trunk, Romania); 4) a truly bizarre electronic combination of Kronos with Charles Ives singing and playing the piano on his song "They are there!", with its subtext "Fighting for the People's New Free World" and dates of composition during World War I and revision during World War II; and 5) the Shostakovich String Quartet no. 8, dedicated "to the victims of fascism and war" (Yaple 1990).[21] The striking contrast of the technical display on "Black Angels," with its own invocation of a consort of viols and references to Schubert's "Death and the Maiden," alongside the primitive yet powerful recordings of the folk songs and the comic yet heartfelt version of the Ives song, balanced by the austere Tallis piece and the introspective Shostakovich work, yields an unlikely but highly affecting collection.[22]

The political themes of *Black Angels* and *Night Prayers* have counterparts in four other releases. Terry Riley's "Salome Dances for Peace," from which an excerpt "Half-Wolf Dances Mad in Moonlight" appeared earlier (*WwH*), is an extended work in five sections. Originally conceived as a ballet, the scenario concerns the return of Salome, 2000 years later, at the summons of the Great Spirit, to fight the dark forces that have stolen peace from the world. Riley combines stories and symbols from ancient myths, biblical legend, and Native American culture, along with a distinctly feminist subtext that requires Salome, the embodiment of the feminist force, to save the world from the masculine war demons. The accompanying music combines "jazz, blues, North Indian raga, Middle Eastern scales, Minimalist pattern, and traditional Western art music" (Swed 1989, 4).[23] The overwhelming impression is of an epic story, told in a series of vignettes, with an overriding musical structure based partly on recurring melodic/motivic materials and on the uniformity of the harmonic language in defined sections that punctuate the diverse styles.

In a second political release, Steve Reich's "Different Trains" harkens back to his earlier tape pieces, in that "speech recordings generate the musical material" (Reich 1989). Reich combines the live group with three recordings, all mixed together to yield up to sixteen parts, overlaid with repeating recorded text fragments and train sounds. The text and context concern Reich's own travels on the train as a young boy at the same time that Nazi trains in Europe carried millions of Jews to their deaths. The music is largely constructed of the pulsating, repetitive motives in consecutive formal blocks characteristic of many of Reich's pieces, and stemming from classical minimalism.

On the CD devoted to "All the Rage" by Bob Ostertag, the piece is an electronic combination of the Kronos quartet and taped crowd noises and added text (by Sara Miles), with the program stemming from riots in San Francisco that followed Governor Wilson's vetoed bill designed to protect gays and lesbians from discrimination (Ostertag 1993). In this openly political recording, with a pink triangle on the CD itself, Kronos donated their royalties to the American Foundation for AIDS Research. The piece is in three parts, each beginning with the voice alone intoning part of the text (0′ 0″, 7′ 31″, and 12′ 54″), and the end marked by a long solo viola soliloquy. Among many remarkable moments are the melting of the crowd noise into string harmonies (6′ 56″) and the transferring of the beating heart of the narrator to the physical beating of the protesters at the hands of the police.

Finally, in the combined electronic manipulation of a speech by I. F. Stone along with string quartet by Scott Johnson (*SS*), the Kronos quartet makes an explicitly political statement about the world and the problems between peoples and nations. In this respect — the political themes of recordings — Kronos follows the lead of rock, folk, and country musicians such as Peter Gabriel, Sting, Bob Geldoff, and Willie Nelson, who have supported political and social causes, and continues the activist spirit leading from the 1960s to productions like "Live Aid" — a spirit quite foreign to traditional classical chamber music. This social conscience is undoubtedly another feature that allows Kronos to attract the baby boomer audience.

Eclectic Trends: Tangos, Jazz, Variations, Electronics, Postmodernism, and Quotation

Possibly the most consistently heard commentary on the Kronos Quartet concerns their eclectic tastes, as reflected in their recordings and concerts.

As I discuss further below, this openness to many different kinds of contemporary music is crucial to the crumbling of boundaries that has followed in the group's wake. The iconoclastic nature of the compilation on *Kronos Quartet* compilation returns on *White Man Sleeps* and *Winter Was Hard*, with an increase in numbers of pieces from six to eight to ten. The Volans piece "White man Sleeps" and Hassell's "pano da Costa" ("Cloth from the Coast") continue the world-minimalist textures of the Sculthorpe quartet. The Hassell work in particular features the alternation of long-note duet melody sections with faster, rhythmic passages over accompanying drones characteristic of the two minimalist-related textures described above. Both the "Morango...Almost a Tango" (by Thomas Oboe Lee) and "Lonely Woman" (by Ornette Coleman) also feature a texture related both to minimalism and to the variation forms described below: a long melody over a repeating, ostinato bass construction. The Tango begins a trend that continues on *Winter Was Hard* with the "Four, for Tango" by Astor Piazzola and a subsequent CD single *Five Tango Sensations* with Piazzola. Although Piazzola has combined jazz and Italian opera with Tango elements to create an "art music" *Nuevo Tango* (new Tango), Ken Hunt notes that the Tango "was the music of rebellion for a sub-class" and it "began in the whorehouses of Argentina and moved on to the world's concert halls" (Hunt 1991).[24] The inclusion of the Tango in the Kronos repertoire is thus linked with the political themes outlined above.

The Ornette Coleman piece links Kronos to its own past — the early albums of music by Bill Evans and Thelonius Monk, on which Kronos worked with producers, arrangers, and performers associated with these two jazz giants. The word jazz also brings up an interesting issue with the group. One of the traits commonly associated with jazz is, of course, improvisation, with varying strictures provided by harmony and rhythm as dictated by the conventions of style. The members of Kronos don't improvise, as a conscious choice from the beginning, but always play from scores; in so doing they left the door open for the Turtle Island Quartet, who distinguish themselves through their improvisations (Heffley 1991). In response to questions regarding improvisation, David Harrington instead stresses interpretation:

What we tried to do on the Monk record is find those performances that we thought were just the most magnificent ones and then work with them as the basis of our notated music. . . . I'm not as interested in 'jamming.' I'm more interested in the highly considered, essential thought that has gone through the essence of a person's life and comes out as a statement that can be something we can all work with and find ways of relating to at various times and places . . . in terms of Kronos, we find our interpretation of the music by visiting it many different times, in different places, and different circumstances, and I value that a lot, and I look at the art of music notation as something that really only tells part of the story. I think of our music as something that is mainly a verbal tradition. (Harrington 1995)

Despite the choice not to improvise but work from the notated score, Harrington's closing remark here indicates that interpretation for Kronos creates a "verbal tradition," a closeness the group fosters between themselves and composers as they collaborate.[25] Aside from the somewhat jazz-like *Bella by Barlight* by John Lurie (*WwH*), Kronos has not returned to the world of jazz music on their recordings. By not improvising, Kronos links itself strongly with the classical chamber-music tradition, which is score-based and differentiates itself from popular-music ensembles, whether jazz, rock, or folk, in which some level of improvisation is always involved (Shumway 1992, 121). Yet, in their stress on interpretation that draws the group into the realm of the composer — who is often close by — Kronos defines a unique space for itself in the world of chamber groups by focusing on the preparation and presentation of contemporary music; and only in contemporary music is such close interaction with the composer possible.

Another recurring feature of Kronos recordings is updated versions of variation forms. In the Sallinen piece, "String Quartet no. 3: Some Aspects of Peltoniemi Hintrik's Funeral March" (*KQ*), the theme, a Finnish fiddler's tune, is subject to various contortions and distortions supplied by the accompaniment, but it is retained through the pointillism, effects, and drones to survive into a relatively romantic ending. A similar setting of "Amazing Grace" (Ben Johnston) appears on *White Man Sleeps*, and the form returns periodically, as on *Night Prayers* in "A Cool Wind Is Blowing" (Tigram Tahmizyan) and "K'Vakarat" (Osvaldo Golijov). This form of distorting variations on a familiar tune might itself be regarded as a metaphor for the Kronos adaptation of the traditional string quartet. As with the recognizable tune in these variations, throughout the Kronos recordings, this familiar string quartet medium is stretched and strained, and found in unlikely and unexpected circumstances that reveal more about its true nature than was hitherto expected.

In discussion above, I noted that *Forbidden Fruit* (*WwH*) by John Zorn, which combines the live Kronos quartet with tape, text, and turntables in a pastiche of music, noise, styles, and times presented tongue-in-cheek, is the closest Kronos comes to postmodernism. The effect derives not only within the piece in and of itself, but in its immediate and jarring proximity to the preceding Webern "Bagatelles, Opus 9," which present the atonal expressionist aspect of the modernist aesthetic in its most condensed and — particularly in the Kronos version — impassioned form. The style of the Zorn work, which stems from the various paths in electronic music and the tradition of combining live and taped instruments, is also strongly indebted to the popular-music world, especially pieces like the Beatles "Revolution no. 9" (*The Beatles "White Album"*) and, in its use of turntables, rap music. The format of electronic compilation returns repeatedly in the Kronos repertoire, on the humorous "A Door Is Ajar" (*WwH*, recalling the Beatles's "Her Majesty" on *Abbey Road*), "Doom A Sigh" and "They are there" (*BA*), "All the Rage" (*BO:AR*), and "Spectre," "Soliloquy from How It Happens (The Voice of I. F. Stone)," and Zorn's own "Cat O' Nine Tails (Tex Avery Directs the Marquis de Sade)" (*SS*), which continues the spirit of his earlier piece.

The Zorn pieces share with several others the use of quotation, which is often cited as an element of postmodernism in music but is actually a venerable historical practice in both the classical and popular worlds, extending throughout recorded history. In Zorn's music, the quotes are indiscriminate "found" objects from history, with apparently no particular meaning within an established context. In the Crumb "Black Angels," however, the appearance of the theme from Schubert's "Death and the Maiden" and the "Dies Irae," along with the number symbolism around 3, 7, and 13, are significant programmatic elements, specifically chosen to fit into an overall structural unity. Similar uses of quotations, although with varying levels of participation in an overall structure, are found in Ives's "Scherzo" (*WMS*), the Schnittke "String Quartet no. 3" (*WwH*) and the Górecki pieces.[26] A more generalized version of quotation, in the stylistic recreation of Medieval and Renaissance-era sounds of viols and expansive textures framed by austere counterpoint, links "Fratres" by Arvo Pärt, the Schnittke "String Quartet no. 3" (*WwH*), Crumb's "Black Angels" (particularly Images 6 and 8), and Górecki's "Already it is Dusk." The texture prevades the Pärt work; in the Schnittke and Górecki pieces the thin consort texture returns throughout linking sections; and in the Crumb piece it appears as part of the "Death and the Maiden" reference. Only in the Schnittke piece, however, is there any sense of stylistic discontinuity or postmodern mixing of genres. Pärt's music is stylistically homogenous, Crumb integrates the ancient timbres with quotation securely fastened on an overall organic conception, and Górecki, as in his "Quasi una Fantasia" in which the movements are unified by a pulse of varying tempi, character, and articulation, creates in "Already it is Dusk" an integral structure of bittersweet consonance and struggling dissonance that might be labeled "medieval modernist."

The eclectic compilation form of Kronos's first three releases, which largely defined the group for their audience and the media, has actually been superceded by the thematic and single composer/piece-based releases that followed. The original form returns, however, and is brought into sharp relief on *Short Stories*, a collection which strains at the boundaries of a single CD as Kronos itself pulls at the conventional notions of a string quartet. While the hallmark of successful popular music artists in the 1980s and 1990s has been the ability to recreate and transform styles and images with each new release — a process which

Kronos follows — the stylistic diversity on *Short Stories* is unprecedented in the popular and classical worlds. Virtually all stylistic avenues previously explored by the group are present: an experiment in effects recreating the sound of the quartet as a typewriter in Elliot Sharp's "Digital"; the American/British blues/rock cover tradition on Willie Dixon's "Spoonful"; electronic music sound manipulation and recombination on John Oswald's "Spectre"; a postmodern electronic collage on John Zorn's "Cat O' Nine Tails"; a progressive modernist composition on Henry Cowell's "Quartet Euphometric"; a "contemporary modernist" piece with electric guitar, "Physical Property" by Steven Mackey; the political electronic combination "Soliloquy from How It Happens (The Voice of I. F. Stone)" by Scott Johnson; the abstract modernist "String Quartet no. 2" by Sofia Gubaidulina; and the world/Indian music composition "Aba kee tayk hamaree" by the Pakistani composer Pandit Pran Nath, complete with voice, tabla and tamboura. This remarkable recording strains conventional musical and social boundaries to the breaking point, leaving only the chronological boundary of the present age.

Conclusion: Dualism, Belief, and Boundaries

The return of the eclectic compilation on *Short Stories* in the midst of the separate, unified releases featuring works by composers Górecki, Feldman, and Glass, and the unified nationalist collection *Night Prayers*, points up the dualistic nature of the Kronos Quartet. On the one hand, the group is committed to diversity and renewal: in this regard, Harrington has noted that Kronos is continually experimenting with orders and combinations of pieces, as "one way we learn more about our own material" (Harrington 1995). On the other hand, Kronos is devoted to interpreting the music and composers that act, in Harrington's words (1995), as "magnets" to which the quartet can anchor itself. One important magnet for the group has been the composers associated with minimalism in its varied forms, and I have attempted to relate their wide-ranging exploration of world music to the musical features world musics share with minimalism. Another magnet for the group is the codification of modernist, twentieth-century masterworks; Kronos has both participated in the celebration of great works from this century and contributed in an essential way to the creation of new "great" works.

Terry Riley, a seminal influence on the Kronos Quartet, uses the same image of "magnetism" in reference to the quartet but coupled with a spiritual component to describe the "strongly felt spiritual attraction [that] has bonded the group energy of the quartet" (Riley 1989). This added dimension is an important one when considering the Kronos phenomenon. In assessing the Kronos's output to date and especially in conversation with David Harrington, the impression arises that the spiritual aspect of the group amounts to a belief in contemporary music that borders on the mystical. Such belief in the musical present and future is not only often lacking, but is actually replaced by active disbelief and rejection, even among otherwise devoted musicians. With regard to repertoire and personal taste, Harrington admits only the chronological boundaries of the current age; in a time of minimalism, electronic technology, postmodernism, and world music amidst a growing canon of "masterworks" from the century, these labels define Kronos's music only insofar as they are of the present:

It's amazing how the sound [of the String Quartet] has begun to appear in various settings and different places, musicians are thinking about the quartet as a vital active medium of music; there's very few composers that I've met in the last ten years that don't want to write a quartet piece. I think the personal aspect to this music and to the way it's prepared is something that is really appealing to people right now . . . Music is something musicians share with each other. I feel the need to explore and expand what I'm hearing. For me it's a searching for definitions of what it is to be a musician every day. It changes; things are very different from 1973. There's so many ways our work can go; I'm looking for those ways that feel like it has to be that way . . . that you can say "yes" for yourself, and I'm sure that there's many things that the next step could be . . . People think about these different areas and boundaries; my ear doesn't work that way, for me there are some kinds of experiences that are like magnets, when I find one of those, I become attached to it, and it could come from anywhere. I never know where it's going to come from. I just want to be ready. (Harrington 1995)

Viewed from the outside, the Kronos Quartet has created a legacy remarkable for its success and renewal in an area — classical music — that has been troubled in its relation to society for most of this century. The question of exactly what "is really appealing to people right now" is a crucial one, however. Kronos has been bold in its mode of presentation to break the mold of classical chamber music groups by doing something rather simple: looking and performing as if they live today rather than somewhere back in history, in terms of their wardrobe as well as their repertoire. Combined with a high level of integrity and musicianship, and a devotion to the music of the time, this mode of presentation has an unmistakable ring of sincerity about it. Performers and promoters of rock music have demonstrated time and again the importance of this link of a sincere belief with their audiences; no amount of promoting can overcome a loss of faith. The Kronos Quartet has shown that, with this faith, the boundaries of music can be reduced to chronological ones, rather than national, social, or educational barriers. This re-drawing of a single large boundary around many smaller existing ones is a lesson important for the future of music.

References

Beadle, Jeremy. 1993. "No Strings". *Music Magazine* (July).

Bornoff, Jack. 1973. "Five Interviews: Pierre Boulez". *Cultures: Music and Society* 1/1: 123.

Bruce, Keith. 1994. "Rocking Old Roles". *Glasgow Herald* (July 20).

Chasins, Abram. 1972. *Music at the Crossroads*. New York: MacMillan.

Classical Music: "It's Cool Again". 1992. *Billboard* 104/38 (September 19): 3.

DeCurtis, Anthony, ed. 1992. *Present Tense: Rock & Roll and Culture*. Durham: Duke University Press.

Dixon Willie and Snowden, Don. 1989. *I Am the Blues*. London: Quartet Books; reprinted by Da Capo Press.

Elson, John. 1989. "Fanatic Champions of the New: The Kronos Quartet Has a Mod Look — and a Mod Repertoire". *Time* 133 (June 26): 86.

Fisk, Josiah. 1991. "An Audience Speaks up: From the Bottom of a Rowboat in a Swamp". *Chamber Music* 8/3 (Fall): 9ff.

Fried, Stephen. 1989. "Classical Flash". *Gentlemen's Quarterly* 59 (September): 240.

Frith, Simon, ed. 1989. *World Music, Politics and Social Change*. Manchester: Manchester University Press.

Gass, Glenn. 1992. "Why Don't We Do It in the Classroom?", in DeCurtis 1992: 93–100.

Goldberg, Joe. 1992. "The New Chamber Music". *Billboard* 104 (September 19): 4.

Gordon, Diane. 1994. "Play it". *Strings* 9/1, issue 43 (July/August): 30ff.

Hamm, Charles. 1989. "Afterword", in Frith 1989, 211–16.

Harrington, David. 1995. Telephone Interview with Dave Headlam (30 March).

Hartwell, Robin. 1993. "Postmodernism and Art Music", in Miller 1993, 27–51.

Hatch, David and Millward, Stephen. 1987. *From Blues to Rock: An Analytical History of Pop Music*. Manchester: Manchester University Press.

Headlam, Dave. 1996. "Does the Song Remain the Same? Issues of Authorship and Identification in the Music of Led Zeppelin", in *Concert Music, Rock, and Jazz*, ed. Betsy Marvin and Richard Hermann, 313–63. Rochester: University of Rochester Press.

Heffley, Mike. 1991. "Turtle Island String Quartet: String Savers of American Music?" *Chamber Music* 8/1 (Spring).

Homfray, Tim. 1988. "Kronos Kultur". *The Strad* 99/1175 (March): 220ff.

Hunt, Ken. 1991. Liner Notes. On Kronos Quartet, *Five Tango Sensations*. Elektra Entertainment 79254.

Jepson, B. 1986. "In the Hands of Kronos, The String Quartet Comes Up to Date". *Connoisseur* 216/898: 86.

Keepnews, Orrin. 1985. "Liner Notes. On Kronos Quartet", *Monk Suite*. Landmark Records LCD 1505–2.

The Kronos Quartet. 1993. *Newsmakers* 1.

MacMillan, Rick. 1994. "Editorial: Should Classical Music Be Made Easy?" *Classical Music Magazine* 17/5 (November–December): 5.

Matthews, David. 1989. "Peter Schulthorpe at 60". *Tempo* 170 (September).

Miller, Simon. 1993. *The Last Post*. Manchester: Manchester University Press.

Morgan, Robert, ed. 1993. *Modern Times: From World War I to the Present*. Englewood Cliffs: Prentice Hall.

Naumann. B. 1985. Music in the Present Tense (The Kronos Quartet of San Francisco). *Neue Zeitschrift fur Musik* 146/3.

Ostertag, Bob. 1993. Liner Notes. On Kronos Quartet, *All the Rage*. Elektra 79332.

Pendergast, Mark. 1992. "When Tallis Met Hendrix". *New Statesman & Society* 5 (March 6): 43.

Potter, Keith. 1993. "The Current Musical Scene", in Morgan 1993, 349–87.

Ray, Robert. B. 1992. "Tracking", in DeCurtis 1992, 135–48.

Reich, Steve. 1989. Different Trains. Liner notes on Steve Reich, *Different Trains, Electric Counterpoint*. Elektra / Asylum / Nonesuch Records 79176.

Rice, Hugh Collins. 1989. "Further Thoughts on Schnittke". *Tempo* 168 (March): 13.

Rich, Alan. 1992. "Out of Africa, With Highbrow Violins". *Entertainment* (Friday, February 28).

Richardson, Derek. 1989. "Improvisation with Strings Attached". *Chamber Music* 6/2 (Summer): 14ff.

Richardson, Susan. 1992. "Review of Pieces of Africa". *Rolling Stone* 628 (April 16): 86.

Riley, Terry. 1989. Liner Notes. On Kronos Quartet, *Terry Riley, Salome Dances for Piece*. Elektra Entertainment 79217.

Roos, James. 1989. "New Music America Festival". *Musical America* 109 (May): 32.

Rothstein, Edward. 1987. "The Zeitgeist Quartet". *The New Republic* 197 (October 5): 29.

Royer, Mary Piage. 1989. "Classical Gasp". *American Demographics* 11 (August): 46.

Saakana, Amonsaba, 1993. "African Musical Universe in Western Musical Culture", in Miller 1993.

Sandow, Gregory. 1986. Liner Notes. On Kronos Quartet, *Kronos Quartet*. Elektra / Asylum / Nonesuch Records 79111.

Shumway, David. 1992. "Rock and Roll as Cultural Practice", in DeCurits 1992, 117–34.

Stanton, David. 1985. "Kronos on the Contemporary Frontier". *Chamber Music* 2/2 (Summer): 10ff.

Stark, Phyllis. 1991. "Labels Playing Up Contemporary Look of Classical Acts". *Billboard* 103 (May 4): 1.

Stearns, David Patrick. 1988. "Kronos Quartet". *Stereo Review* 53 (December): 96.

Stewart, Andrew. 1993. "Age of the Titans". *Classical Music* (July 17).

Strickland, Edward. 1993. *Minimalism: Origins*. Bloomington: Indiana University Press.

Sussman, Deborah. 1988. "The Kronos Quartet". *Scholastic Update* 120 (May 20): 32.

Swed, Mark. 1989. Liner Notes. On Kronos Quartet, *Terry Riley, Salome Dances for Peace*. Elektra 79217.

Tenzer, Michael. 1993. "Western Music in the Context of World Music", in Morgan 1993, 388–410.

Terry, Ken. 1992a. "Kronos Foursome Enjoying a Double Chart Success". *Billboard* 104/21 (May 23): 8.

Terry, Ken. 1992b. "Pieces of Africa". *Billboard* 104/21 (May 23): 8.

Tesser, Neil. 1987. "The New Fab Four". *Rolling Stone* (May 7): 16.

Théberg, Paul. 1993. "Random Access: Music, Technology, Postmodernism", in Miller 1993, 150–82.

Ulrich, Allan. 1989. "New Releases from John Adams and the Kronos". *San Francisco Examiner* (November 17).

Waffender, "Manfred, director. 1993". *About 4*. Tempomedia, Euroarts International.

Wallace, H. 1993. Concertos (The Kronos-Quartet and the Balanescu-Quartet have Transformed That Most Exclusive Traditional of European Art-Forms into the Coolest Show in Town). *Strad* 104/1233 (January): 70.

Wilcox, Brent. 19?? "The Kronos Quartet — Playing Music from Bartok to Zappa Erases the Dividing Lines Between Jazz, Rock, and Classical". *Downbeat* 54/5: 55–57.

Yanov-Yanovsky, Dmitri. 1994. Lacrymosa. Liner notes On Kronos Quartet, *Night Prayers*. Elektra 79346.

Yaple, Carol. 1994. Liner Notes. On Kronos Quartet, *Black Angels*. Elektra 79242.

Young, Marcia. 1991. "Different Trains of Thought". *The Strad* 102/1219 (November): 998.

Notes

1. Kronos's CD *Pieces of Africa* was the first to be ranked no. 1 on both the Billboard classical and world music charts. See Terry 1992a, wherein an agent for Kronos's label, Nonesuch, notes that *"Pieces of Africa* [was pitched] to classical, world music, and pop markets 'to whatever extent possible'" and that "This album has been covered by pop press from the day of release, and the world music market is a subset of the pop market."

2. My information on the quartet comes from the sources cited throughout this article, liner notes to the recordings, and from a phone conversation with David Harrington on 30 March 1995. Most writers note the chamber group Tashi as one forerunner of Kronos, but also point to an Atlantic release from 1964, *A Quartet is a Quartet is a Quartet*, featuring the Modern Jazz Quartet, the Quartetto di Milano (playing music of Webern), and a Hungarian Gypsy Quartet, which thus combines jazz, "ethnic" or world music, and contemporary music at this early date.

3. See, for instance, Fisk 1991, Heffley 1991, and Richardson 1989. For an extended treatment of the "problems" with classical music dating from the early 1970s, see Chasins 1972.

4. A trip to the local classical music section at CD outlets reveals the inventive although sometimes unintentionally hilarious recent approaches of classical promoters: 1) music that is sensual, "for lovers," with lots of skin and passionate embraces; 2) the "Beloved" or favorite hits of the classics; 3) functional arrangements, as in a ready-made selection for a dinner party; 4) "New Age" exotic, as in the recent chant revival; 5) the "superstars" or celebrity approach, stemming from Leonard Bernstein and continuing with the ubiquitous Three Tenors; 6) comedy and parody, notably P. D. Q. Bach; 7) a rock 'n' roll inspired "Mad about" approach (from Deutsche Grammaphon no less!); 8) the now classic "for people who hate" approach to classical music; 9) movie-inspired releases, such as *Amadeus* and *Immortal Beloved*, including T-shirts, coffee mugs, etc.; and 10) How-to instructional approaches, such as *Closet Conductor*.

5. Kronos' appeal may also be understood more simply, as Alan Rich (1992) notes, "the Kronos folks always seem to be having fun."

6. The exception is opera, where a single great performer like Luciano Pavoratti can act as the unifying thread, see Shumway 1992, 128.

7. It is interesting to note in this regard that Kronos has not released a video, which would seem to be a natural use of technology and marketing for the group. Harrington noted that they had created a video, but had not released it, and that the decision for another video would be very music-based. Despite their visual appeal, Kronos thus differs — at least on this point — from contemporary popular music by emphasizing only the aural aspect of their music in their releases.

8. In Terry 1992b Harrington replies to an inquiry about performing works from *Pieces of Africa*: "Some of the pieces . . . were recorded just for the album. . . . All of the other pieces we play in concert just as solo pieces [for quartet]. If the composers are there, we perform with them as well."

9. The comparison of Kronos with the Beatles, who stopped touring when they could not recreate their music live, falters at this point.

10. A column of title "short forms" is also given in Figure 1; where I make multiple references to individual pieces and their source CDs, I will use these short forms in parentheses to clarify the references. The list is inclusive to 1995.

11. A complete list of Kronos recordings is difficult to compile, but I count eighteen releases (to 1995) in which they appear on at least one track, ranging from Lou Harrison, John Anthony Lennon, and David Byrne to Gloria Coates and Kaija Saariaho, with many CRI releases, and including at least one award, the American Academy and Institute of Arts and Letters Award for Dane Rudhyar, *Advent: Crisis and Overcoming* (CRI SD 418, 1979).

12. It is interesting and perhaps surprising to note in this regard that Harrington grew up with the traditional classical quartet music of Haydn, Mozart and Beethoven. George Crumb's "Black Angels" was, however, a seminal influence, as Harrington comments: "When I think back to what prompted me to start the group, originally it had to do with an experience I had listening to the radio one night and hearing 'Black Angels' by George Crumb, and that was a very strong experience for me, it felt like all of a sudden I'd found my music," and "when I heard Black Angels it was a mind-boggling experience, it really changed everything for me" (Harrington 1995).

13. In conversation, Harrington (1995) disavowed any conscious invocation of a postmodernist attitude or influence in his choice of music for Kronos.

14. For somewhat comprehensible discussions of postmodernism in contemporary music, see Hartwell 1993 and Théberge 1993.

15. See Hartwell 1993 for a discussion of postmodernism and art music. Briefly, Hartwell groups modernism and the avant garde together in terms of their shared awareness of

history and relationship of art and an age. Postmodernism occurs when the attitude shifts toward appropriation, and language becomes characterized by distortion, fragmentation, and a distancing between sign and meaning.

16. The first recording by Kronos from 1979, re-released on CD by Reference Recordings, is a hybrid combination of new pieces written for Kronos, but with many obvious derivatives of popular styles, using blues patterns and traditional song forms. The change from this recording to the Elektra releases indicates that, as they developed, Kronos consciously moved away from repackaged popular music for the string quartet.

17. There is another interesting relationship between Dixon and Hendrix here; Hendrix went to the United Kingdom in 1967 and became enormously popular in a trio with two white British musicians. His success and band situation, possible through the thriving blues-based rock scene in England which revered figures like Willie Dixon, would not have been possible had he stayed in the States. See Hatch and Millward 1987.

18. For instance, Dixon successfully sued Led Zeppelin for royalties to the songs "I Can't Quit You Baby" and "Whole Lotta Love," the latter derived from his own "You Need Love." See Dixon 1989 and Headlam 1996.

19. Harrington (1995) disavows any conscious intention of combining minimalist and world musics, noting that Kronos had worked with the major figures associated with minimalism — although his personal experience of these composers as individuals was so unique that he found the label meaningless — and had intentionally sought out composers from different parts of the world, but had made no connection between them. World music influences appear, of course, in the music of many composers; see Tenzer 1993, who includes Olivier Messaien, Henry Cowell, Harry Partsch, and many others.

20. For a view on the transformations African music has undergone in its popular music manifestations, see Saakana 1993. An interesting aspect of the question of "authenticity" and the American adoption of "world music" emerged in an interview with Kronos's Harrington and composer Dumisani Maraire on NPR (broadcast 28 February 1992). The interviewer (Julie Burstein) noted reviews characterizing *Pieces of Africa* as "ersatz folk music," to which Maraire responded that "the same discussions are taking place in Africa." When Maraire took *Pieces of Africa* back to Zimbabwe and played it for the principal of a junior college of music, where only classical and jazz music was taught, the principal asked if this was "the new style in the American States jazz" and Maraire replied, laughing "[No] It is Shona." The interview ends noting that Maraire "has just opened the first school to teach traditional Shona music in Zimbabwe." Such realities underscore the arguments of Hamm and Frith.

21. With regard to the Ives's piece, in Beadle 1993 Harrington notes that "Ives had indicated optional violins in the accompaniment, so John Geist wrote us an arrangement."

22. Harringon has noted that the *Black Angels* collection "was constructed so that everything seemed to have its part within the whole, where everything belonged in a way that could readily be perceived" (Stewart 1993).

23. In an evocative juxtaposition, Allan Ulrich (1989) describes Riley's cycle as a "minimalist tone-poem."

24. In the early part of this century the tango also found its way into Europe and was used by many composers, as in the Viennese composer Alban Berg's use of the Tango as a symbol of decay and decadence in his concert aria *Der Wein* as well as in his second opera, *Lulu*.

25. Harrington's comments in this regard clarify an otherwise obscure statement by Orrin Keepnews on the Monk recording (Keepnews 1985): "These four musicians [Kronos] are not, and do not seek to be, improvising artists. What they do, superbly well, is to *interpret* the written material, which is as much a matter of individual and collective

emotional reaction and understanding as it is of technique. It is a good deal closer to the aims and achievements of improvisation than many jazz people might realize, although it does call for much greater respect for the composer and a lot less license in dealing with his creation than is customary in jazz."

26. See Rice 1989 for Schnittke; Rice notes the references to a Lassus Stabat Mater, the theme of Beethoven's "Grosse Fuge," and Shostakovich's signature pitch set D-Eb-C-B (DSCH) in this piece.

Contemporary Music Review
2000, Vol. 19, Part 1, pp. 141–142
Reprints available directly from the publisher
Photocopying permitted by license only

Can Music Reweave the Fabric of Our Fragmented Culture?

William Bolcom

It has been said that serious composers ignore popular music at their own peril. I've always felt that way. In our still-maturing American culture popular music has been — with the movies — the defining essence of our national style. I say *has been* because my fear is that, right now, the movies and pop music have become Big Business to such a degree that it all isn't really popular art anymore. Too often they are the result of market research and manipulation; too often they are cynically thrown at a public that has lost the ability to discern because of so many years of nurturance toward a state of pure appetite.

Any music of worth involves participation on all fronts, from performer to creator and listener. The doctors' string quartets at the height of Viennese musical culture and the garage bands of the rock era shared one thing: Never mind about the quartet or the band being any good or not; what these disparate musical cultures had in common was a participant's interest in the world of music from which these pieces arose.

A passive listener is not a listener. We need to reintroduce the concept of audience. How do we link members of an audience together? people whose contact is mostly with a screen and hardly with each other? Music can fill a physical need; there is definitely a druglike music wherein the vibrations produce a desired result within the human body, almost without passing through the ear or brain. We all know, however, that music can do much more for us. But in order for this to be so, we need something of a shared context — and this holds for music in any style — and without an audience one can knit together somehow, music can't get to anything past a basal level.

Maybe this is where rap comes in. Although as exploited as any other branch of pop music, it still smells of the streets. What's intriguing in it is the unusual line lengths, the triplets against the beat, the enjambments in the treatment of the text; when musical notes begin more and more to fit with rap's spoken rhythms, we may have a new sort of popular music. (Perhaps listeners became so tired of being manipulated by musical hooks that they preferred verbal and rhythmic hooks as a change for awhile, and who can blame them?) But another explanation for the absence of music in rap is the fact that musical training of any sort is less and less available to young people today. Add this to the induced passivity of media culture and you have the recipe for the current musical malaise, as well as the societal one. People can't make music together; but then they can't work together on a job together at the moment either (ask any employer about the untrainability of the young).

It is too much to ask music of any sort — popular, classical, "serious," whatever — to help reweave the fabric of our fragmented culture?

Contemporary Music Review
2000, Vol. 19, Part 1, pp. 143–144
Reprints available directly from the publisher
Photocopying permitted by license only

© 2000 OPA (Overseas Publishers Association) N.V.
Published by license under
the Harwood Academic Publishers imprint,
part of The Gordon and Breach Publishing Group.
Printed in Malaysia.

Copyright Notices

Contemporary Music Review
2000, Vol. 19, Part 1, pp. 145–146
Reprints available directly from the publisher
Photocopying permitted by license only

Notes on Contributors

William Bolcom is Ross Lee Finney Distinguished University Professor of Music at the University of Michigan. His broad range of works are widely performed and recorded, and he has recorded twenty albums with his wife, mezzo soprano Joan Morris. Bolcom received the 1988 Pulitzer Prize in Music for his Twelve New Etudes for Piano.

Austin Caswell is Professor Emeritus of Musicology at the School of Music, Indiana University. His most recent publication is *Ornamental Opera Arias* (A-R Edition, 1992).

John Covach is Associate Professor of Music at the University of North Carolina at Chapel Hill. He has published numerous articles on rock music, twelve-tone music, and the philosophy of music. He is Co-Editor (with Graeme Boone) of *Understanding Rock: Essays in Musical Analysis* (Oxford University Press, 1997).

Walter Everett is Associate Professor of Music at the University of Michigan. He has published numerous articles on rock music, art song, opera, Schenkerian theory, and other topics. He is author of *The Beatles as Musicians*: Revolver *through the* Anthology (Oxford University Press, 1999).

Allen Forte is Battell Professor of Music Theory at Yale University, is the author of a number of books and articles. His book, *The American Popular Ballad of the Golden Era 1924–1950* (Princeton University Press, 1995) won the Society for Music Theory's Wallace Berry Book Publication Award in 1997. Yale University Press has recently published his study, *The Atonal Music of Anton Webern*, in the Composers of the Twentieth Century series.

Dave Headlam is Associate Professor of Music Theory at the Eastman School of Music of the University of Rochester. He has published on technology, computers, and music, popular music, and art music of the twentieth century. He is author of *The Music of Alban Berg* (Yale University Press, 1996), which was earned an ASCAP Deems Taylor Award in 1997.

Tama Hochbaum is an artist and graphic designer. She has designed CD covers for a variety of labels, including GM Recordings, Centaur Records, and CRI. She has exhibited her paintings and photographs in New York, Boston and Chapel Hill, North Carolina where she has lived since 1996.

David Joyner is Associate Professor of Music at the University of North Texas in Denton. He has published numerous articles and essays on ragtime and jazz. He is author of the textbook, *American Popular Music* (McGraw-Hill, 1993).

David Neumeyer is Professor and Director of Graduate Studies at the School of Music, Indiana University, Bloomington. His research interests cluster about music between the world wars. He is author of *The Music of Paul Hindemith* (Yale University Press, 1986) and co-editor (with James Buhler and Carol Flynn) of *Music and Cinema* (Wesleyan University Press, forthcoming).

Christopher Smith lectures in world music at Indiana University, where he is completing a Ph.D. in musicology. He is the author of numerous articles on jazz, classical, and world music.

A companion volume to the present one, "American Rock and the Classical Music Tradition" (ed. John Covach and Walter Everett), appears as *Contemporary Music Review* 18/4 (1999).

Contemporary Music Review
2000, Vol. 19, Part 1, pp. 147–153
Reprints available directly from the publisher
Photocopying permitted by license only

© 2000 OPA (Overseas Publishers Association) N.V.
Published by license under
the Harwood Academic Publishers imprint,
part of The Gordon and Breach Publishing Group.
Printed in Malaysia.

Index

NOTES FOR CONTRIBUTORS

Typescripts

Papers should be typed with double spacing on good quality paper and submitted in duplicate to the Editor, **Contemporary Music Review**, c/o Harwood Academic Publishers, at

5th Floor, Reading Bridge House		Po Box 32160		3-14-9, Okubo
Reading Bridge Approach	or	Newark, NJ 07102	or	Shinjuku-ku
Reading RG1 8PP		USA		Tokyo 169
UK				Japan

or directly to the issue editor. Submission of a paper to this journal will be taken to imply that it represents original work not previously published, that it is not being considered elsewhere for publication, and that if accepted for publication it will not be published elsewhere in the same form, in any language, without the consent of the editors and publishers. It is a condition of the acceptance by the editor of a typescript for publication that the publisher acquires automatically the copyright of the typescript throughout the world.

Languages

Papers are accepted only in English.

Abstract

Each paper requires an abstract of 100–150 words summarizing contents

Key words

Up to six key words (index words) should be provided by the author. These will be published at the front of the paper.

Illustrations

All illustrations should be designated as "Figure 1" etc., and be numbered with consecutive arabic numerals. Each illustration should have a descriptive caption and be mentioned in the text. Indicate an approximate position for each illustration in the margin, and note the paper title, the name of the author and the figure number on the back of the illustration (please use a soft pencil for this, not a felt tip pen).

Preparation: All illustrations submitted must be of a high enough standard for direct reproduction. Line drawings should be prepared in black (india) ink on quality white card or paper or on tracing paper, with all the necessary lettering included. Alternatively, good sharp photographs ("glossies") are acceptable. Photographs intended for halftone reproduction must be good, glossy original prints of maximum contrast. Unusable illustrations and example will not be redrawn or retouched by the printer, so it is essential that figures are well prepared.

Musical examples

These, like the illustrations, must be of a high enough standard for direct reproduction. Musical examples should be prepared in black (india) ink on quality white card or white music manuscript paper, or on tracing paper, with any necessary lettering included. If staves are hand drawn, ensure that the lines are of uniform thickness. Unusable musical examples will not be redrawn or retouched by the printer, so it is essential that figures are well prepared.

References and notes

References and notes are indicated in the text by consecutive superior arabic numerals (without parentheses). The full list should be collected and typed at the end of the paper in numerical order. Listed references should be complete in all details, including article titles and journal titles in full. In multiauthor references, the first six authors' names should be listed in full, then "et al" may be used. Examples:

1. Smith, F.J. (1976) Editor. *In Search of Musical Method*, pp. 70–81. New York and London: Gordon and Breach.
2. Cockrell, D. (1982) A study in French Romanticism. *Journal* of *Musicological Research*, 4(1/2), 85–115.

NB: authors must check that reference details are correct and complete; otherwise the references are useless. As a final check, please make sure that references tally with citings in the text.

Proofs

Contributors will receive page proofs (including illustrations) by air mail for correction, which must be returned within 48 hours of receipt. Please ensure that a full postal address is given on the first page of the typescript, so that proofs arrive without delay. Authors' alterations in excess of 10% of the original composition cost will be charged to authors.

Page charges

There are no page charges to individuals or institutions.

INSTRUCTIONS FOR AUTHORS

ARTICLE SUBMISSION ON DISK

The Publisher welcomes submissions on disk. The instructions that follow are intended for use by authors whose articles have been accepted for publication and are in final form. Your adherence to these guidelines will facilitate the processing of your disk by the typesetter. These instructions do not replace the journal Notes for Contributors; all information in Notes for Contributors remains in effect.

When typing your article, do not include design or formatting information. Type all text flush left, unjustified and without hyphenation. Do not use indents, tabs or multi-spacing. If an indent is required, please note it by a line space; also mark the position of the indent on the hard copy manuscript. Indicate the beginning of a new paragraph by typing a line space. Leave one space at the end of a sentence, after a comma or other punctuation mark, and before an opening parenthesis. Be sure not to confuse lower case letter "l" with numeral "1", or capital letter "O" with numeral "0". Distinguish opening quotes from close quotes. Do not use automatic page numbering or running heads.

Tables and displayed equations may have to be rekeyed by the typesetter from your hard copy manuscript. Refer to the journal Notes for Contributors for style for Greek characters, variables, vectors, etc.

Articles prepared on most word processors are acceptable. If you have imported equations and/or scientific symbols into your article from another program, please provide details of the program used and the procedures you followed. If you have used macros that you have created, please include them as well.

You may supply illustrations that are available in an electronic format on a separate disk. Please clearly indicate on the disk the file format and/or program used to produce them, and supply a high-quality hard copy of each illustration as well.

Submit your disk when you submit your final hard copy manuscript. The disk file and hard copy must match exactly.

If you are submitting more than one disk, please number each disk. Please mark each disk with the journal title, author name, abbreviated article title and file names.

Be sure to retain a back-up copy of each disk submitted. Pack your disk carefully to avoid damage in shipping, and submit it with your hard copy manuscript and complete Disk Specifications form (see reverse) to the person designated in the journal Notes for Contributors.

GORDON AND BREACH PUBLISHERS • **HARWOOD ACADEMIC PUBLISHERS**

Disk Specifications

Journal name _____

_____

Date _____ Paper Reference Number _____

Paper title _____

_____

_____

Corresponding author _____

Address _____

_____

_____

_____ Postcode _____

Telephone _____

Fax _____

E-mail _____

Disks Enclosed (file names and descriptions of contents)

Text

Disk 1 _____

Disk 2 _____

Disk 3 _____

PLEASE RETAIN A BACK-UP COPY OF ALL DISK FILES SUBMITTED.

GORDON AND BREACH PUBLISHERS   •   HARWOOD ACADEMIC PUBLISHERS

Figures

Disk 1 _____

Disk 2 _____

Disk 3 _____

Computer make and model _____

_____

Size/format of floppy disks

☐ 3.5"   ☐ 5.25"

☐ Single sided   ☐ Double sided

☐ Single density   ☐ Double density   ☐ High density

Operating system _____

Version _____

Word processor program _____

Version _____

Imported maths/science program _____

Version _____

Graphics program _____

Version _____

Files have been saved in the following format

Text: _____

Figures: _____

Maths: _____

PLEASE RETAIN A BACK-UP COPY OF ALL DISK FILES SUBMITTED.

GORDON AND BREACH PUBLISHERS   •   **HARWOOD ACADEMIC PUBLISHERS**

Made in the USA
Coppell, TX
21 June 2021